top-down
knit sweaters

top-down knit sweaters

16 Versatile Styles
Featuring Texture,
Lace, Cables,
and Colorwork

CORRINA
FERGUSON

**STACKPOLE
BOOKS**

Guilford, Connecticut

Published by Stackpole Books
An imprint of The Rowman & Littlefield Publishing Group, Inc.
4501 Forbes Blvd., Ste. 200
Lanham, MD 20706
www.stackpolebooks.com

Distributed by NATIONAL BOOK NETWORK
800-462-6420

Technical Editors
Heather Anne Zoppetti
Britt Schmiesing

Photography
Corrina Ferguson

Models
Lauren Trumbull
Christine Tran
Scarlett de Luna Medina
Journey Jarrett

British Library Cataloguing in Publication Information available

Library of Congress Cataloging-in-Publication Data available

Names: Ferguson, Corrina, author.
Title: Top-down knit sweaters : 16 versatile styles featuring texture, lace, cables, and colorwork / Corrina Ferguson.
Description: Guilford, Connecticut : Stackpole Books, [2019] | Includes index.
Identifiers: LCCN 2019014924 (print) | LCCN 2019015280 (ebook) | ISBN 9780811768832 (electronic) | ISBN 9780811718288 (pbk. : alk. paper)
Subjects: LCSH: Knitting. | Sweaters. | Shawls.
Classification: LCC TT825 (ebook) | LCC TT825 .F447 2019 (print) | DDC 746.43/2—dc23
LC record available at https://lccn.loc.gov/2019014924

♾™ The paper used in this publication meets the minimum requirements of American National Standard for Information Sciences—Permanence of Paper for Printed Library Materials, ANSI/NISO Z39.48-1992.

First Edition

To my husband Daniel,
who watched me go through
this crazy process yet again and
always supports my insanity.

Contents

CHAPTER 1

Top-Down Tips

Why are top-down sweaters better? Well, it just comes down to one thing—fit. When you knit your sweater in pieces from the bottom up, you can't really try it on. I mean, I guess you could have one of those life-size mannequins that you could pin the pieces to . . . but who really does that? With a top-down sweater, you can put it on waste yarn or long cables and actually try it on, to know that it well and truly fits or to know the sleeves need to be longer (unless you want to show off that wrist tattoo that your grandma doesn't know you have). Also, unless you are a speed demon, knitting a sweater is a huge time investment—not to mention the cost of the materials. So make yourself or your loved one a sweater that fits. Knit it top down.

This book has two kinds of sweaters: raglan and yoke style. What's the difference? Well, in a raglan-style sweater, all the increases are worked along four lines—kind of like your classic old-school baseball T-shirt. With a yoke sweater, you space the increases out evenly around the sweater in order to have a yoke that fits around your shoulders and upper body. Which is easier? Sometimes I think raglans are easier to knit because it's easy to keep track of the increases. But speaking as a designer, yokes are so much easier—especially when you need a sweater that will fit more than one size of human.

I tried to do a good range of sizes for these sweaters. Most of them go from about a 32-inch to a 56-inch / 81.5-cm to a 142-cm finished bust size. What bust size should you knit? How big is your bust? I know, I know, such a personal question. When you measure your bust, please measure the biggest part of your bust—not your bra band, but around the fullest part of your bust. Then decide how tight or loose you want the sweater to be. And then choose a size that is exactly the size of your bust (keeping in mind that knitting is stretchy!) or a few inches smaller or larger, depending on how you want it to fit. If you ever have questions about which size might be best for you, feel free to shoot me an email at corrina@craftstartstudios.com.

And, finally, one of my favorite things about top-down sweaters is the lack of seaming. Really, the only thing you end up seaming is under the arms. And if you are sneaky and pick up your sleeve stitches from the underarm cast-on for the body, you can even avoid that. But I can't help you with the weaving in of ends. That just has to be done.

Needle Notes

What kind of needles should you use for your top-down sweater? First off, and most important, you should use the size that gets you gauge. I don't care if I suggest an 8 and you need a 6. Get gauge! It's so important to make sure your sweater fits that it doesn't matter whether your needle size is wildly different from the suggested one. Your gauge has to work! You want a fabric that you like, of course, but if the gauge doesn't match the pattern, your sweater won't fit.

All of the sweaters in this book have sleeves or sleeve edgings worked in the round. Yes, even the cardigans do, where the body is worked flat. So you need to have access to your favorite method for working small circumferences in the round. Maybe you like dpns (double-pointed needles) or maybe, like me, you prefer magic loop. Use whatever works best for you.

For any pullovers, you will probably need two circular needles, one small enough for the cast-on/neckline area and one that is slightly smaller than your bust size. For example, if you are working a 36-inch / 91.5-cm bust, you will want to use a 32-inch / 81.5-cm circular needle. We don't want your knitting stretched out! You can work the neckline on dpns or magic loop style as well, if you prefer.

For cardigans, I *highly* suggest using circular needles—yes, even for the flat yoke/raglan area and body. Why? Because you are going to have a lot of stitches on those needles, and I really don't think you could manage them on straight needles. Now you may be a knitting magician and can make it work . . . but make it easy on yourself (and your wrists) and use circular needles for knitting flat. The nice thing about the cardigan styles is that you can just pick the one length—again slightly smaller than the bust you are working—and do all the knitting but the sleeves.

I love a good interchangeable set for knitting top-down sweaters! It's nice to be able to switch the cable lengths whenever I want. So grab your favorite circular knitting needles and get started!

Interchangeable Increases

Do you know what all top-down sweaters have in common? There are increases—lots and lots of increases. You start with just neck stitches, and then you increase like crazy until you have enough stitches for almost your entire bust and upper arms, and then there is some knitting magic and you make a sweater—ta-da! But seriously, there is so much increasing. The patterns in this book don't use any super fancy increases, but you can change things up if you like to make the sweater your own.

The following increases are totally interchangeable—you can use them in place of each other, and there are no adjustments needed. *But* it can change the way your sweater looks—a lot!

INCREASES BETWEEN STITCHES

M1 (make 1): Insert LH needle from front to back under horizontal strand between last st worked and next st on LH needle, knit through back of resulting loop—1 st inc'd.

yo (yarn over): Bring yarn to the front, wrap it over the top of the RH needle, and work next stitch.

backward loop: With your right hand, create an "e-loop" with the working yarn on the top of the loop. Then place the loop on the RH needle tip and pull the working yarn to tighten the stitch, creating what looks like a twisted yarn over.

The big difference between the make 1 and the yarn over is that the make 1 is nearly invisible while the yarn over makes a hole, or an eyelet, in your knitting. If you want to close the hole, you can work the yarn over through the back loop on the following row, and it will pretty much close it up. It just depends on what kind of look you are going for. I tend to use yarn over increases on sweaters that have lace or other eyelets in the mix.

Another interchangeable increase you can use in place of these is the backward loop increase—just like a backward loop cast-on. That one is virtually invisible as well.

INCREASES WORKED ON STITCHES

The next set of increases is different. Instead of being worked in between stitches, they are worked on stitches. What that means is that you take one stitch and turn it into more. If you want to substitute a different sort of increase, you would have to account for that stitch. So, for instance, if you want to use a make 1 instead of a kfb, you would have to actually knit the stitch that was supposed to be the kfb, and then work the M1 either before or after that stitch.

kfb: Knit into front and back of same st—1 st inc'd.

pfb: Purl into front and back of same st—1 st inc'd.

kyok (knit, yarn over, knit): (K1, yo, k1) in same st—2 sts inc'd.

When you work the kfb, it basically ends up looking like a knit stitch with a purl bump

nestled right next to it. I really like the kfb increase because it's super easy to make sure you didn't forget an increase. The pfb is a little less obvious.

The kyok increase is very decorative. You end up with three stitches where there used to be one, and with the center stitch being a yarn over, it's a perfect increase in a lace setting. Obviously, kyok would be a little difficult to sub for and could really change the look of things, so you might want to follow the pattern.

The big thing to keep in mind with increases is that if you, say, absolutely hate the standard make 1 increase or the way it looks, you have options!

All about Buttons

Lots of designs in this book call for buttons. So here are a few tips about buttons that might help.

First, choose buttons you love. Buttons are a fun way to show your personality on a sweater.

Love frogs? Make Vivian (see photo) navy and green and add some adorable frog buttons. Fun buttons aren't just for kids!

Second, sew those buttons on with needle and thread. Like actual thread. Not yarn. It would be terrible if you sewed your buttons on with a single-ply yarn that broke and you lost one! Buttonholes are fequently too small for tapestry needles. Needle and thread make it much easier to manage, and they add a layer of security.

Third, you can change the size of the buttons. Now hear me out here. Let's say the sweater calls for ¾-inch / 1.9-cm buttons, but you have some gorgeous larger ones that will make that sweater all yours. Do it! How? Well, you are going to need bigger buttonholes. If your buttonhole is two stitches, then three stitches might be way too big for your larger button. But it's better to make a buttonhole that is a bit too big than too small. You can always use your handy needle and thread to tighten it up a bit if desired. So use the buttons you love!

CHAPTER 2

Tantalizing Texture

Knitting is so much about how it feels—how the yarn feels in your hands, how the sweater feels against your skin. In this chapter, we use knits and purls and slip stitches to incorporate beautiful textures into our knitting without too much fuss.

Auralee

Auralee is a raglan cardigan with two kind of stripes—simple texture stripes in one color and the same stripes echoed in three other colors. It uses only a bit of each of the contrast colors, so it's perfect if you have bits and pieces of a favorite yarn.

SIZE
Bust: 32 (36, 40, 44, 48, 52, 56) in. / 81.5 (91.5, 101.5, 112, 122, 132, 142) cm

YARN
Anzula Cricket; DK weight; 80% wool, 10% nylon, 10% cashmere; 250 yd. / 228 m, 4 oz. / 114 g per skein
   Toffee (MC): 4 (4, 5, 6, 6, 7, 7) skeins
   Candied Apple (CC1): 1 skein
   Peach (CC2): 1 skein

NEEDLES
US 6 (4.0 mm); adjust needle size as necessary to achieve gauge.

NOTIONS
- stitch markers
- tapestry needle
- waste yarn or stitch holders

GAUGE
20 sts and 28 rows = 4 in. / 10 cm in St st

NOTES
All slip stitches are slipped purlwise with the yarn to the WS of the work. The slip stitches in the main color body and sleeve section will always line up.

INSTRUCTIONS

YOKE

With MC, CO 43 (43, 43, 51, 59, 63, 67) sts.
Place Marker Row (WS): K1, p2, pm, p3, pm, p31 (31, 31, 39, 47, 51, 55), pm, p3, pm, p2, k1.

SETUP ROWS

Row 1 (RS): K1, kfb, k1, sm, kfb twice, k1, sm, kfb, knit to 2 sts before next m, kfb, k1, sm, kfb twice, k1, sm, kfb, k2—51 (51, 51, 59, 67, 71, 75) sts.

Row 2 (WS): K1, purl to last st, k1.

Row 3: K1, M1, sl 1, kfb, k1, sm, kfb, k1, sl 1, kfb, k1, sm, kfb, k1, *sl 1, k3; rep from * to 3 sts before next m, sl 1, kfb, k1, sm, kfb, k1, sl 1, kfb, k1, sm, kfb, k1, sl 1, M1, k1—61 (61, 61, 69, 77, 81, 85) sts.

Row 4: Knit to end, slipping all sl sts from the previous row.

Row 5: K1, M1, knit to 2 sts before next m, kfb, k1, (sm, kfb, knit to 2 sts before next m, kfb, k1) 3 times, sm, kfb, knit to last st, M1, k1—71 (71, 71, 79, 87, 91, 95) sts.

Row 6: K1, purl to last st, k1.

RAGLAN PHASE ONE

Raglan Phase One has V-neck and raglan increases. Every RS row has raglan increases, and Rows 3, 7, and 9 have V-neck increases.

Work 24 (34, 34, 44, 54, 64, 64) rows of Raglan Phase One, and then move on to Raglan Phase Two—181 (227, 227, 281, 335, 385, 389) sts; 27 (35, 35, 43, 51, 59, 59) sts for each front, 33 (43, 43, 53, 63, 73, 73) sts for each sleeve, and 61 (71, 71, 89, 107, 121, 125) sts for the back.

Row 1 (RS): Knit to 2 sts before next m, kfb, k1, (sm, kfb, knit to 2 sts before next m, kfb, k1) 3 times, sm, kfb, knit to end—8 sts inc'd.

Row 2 (WS): K1, purl to last st, k1.

Row 3: K1, M1, knit to 2 sts before next m, kfb, k1, (sm, kfb, knit to 2 sts before next m, kfb, k1) 3 times, sm, kfb, knit to last st, M1, k1—10 sts inc'd.

Row 4: Rep Row 2.

Rows 5–6: Rep Rows 1–2.

Row 7: K1, M1, *k3, sl 1; rep from * to 3 sts before next m, k1, kfb, k1, (sm, kfb, k2, sl 1, *k3, sl 1; rep from * to 3 sts before next m, k1, kfb, k1) 3 times, sm, kfb, k2, sl 1, *k3, sl 1; rep from * to last 4 sts, k3, M1, k1—10 sts inc'd.

Row 8: Knit to end, slipping all sl sts from the previous row.

Rows 9–16: Rep Rows 3–4, then work Rows 1–6 once more.

Row 17: K1, M1, k2, sl 1, *k3, sl 1; rep from * to 4 sts before next m, k2, kfb, k1, (sm, kfb, *k3, sl 1; rep from * to 4 sts before next m, k2, kfb, k1) 3 times, sm, kfb, *k3, sl 1; rep from * to last 3 sts, k2, M1, k1—10 sts inc'd.

Row 18: Knit to end, slipping all sl sts from the previous row.

Rows 19–26: Rep Rows 3–4, then work Rows 1–6 once more.

Row 27: K1, M1, k1, sl 1, *k3, sl 1; rep from * to 5 sts before next m, k3, kfb, k1, (sm, kfb, sl 1, *k3, sl 1; rep from * to 5 sts before next m, k3, kfb, k1) 3 times, sm, kfb, sl 1, *k3, sl 1; rep from * to last 2 sts, k1, M1, k1—10 sts inc'd.

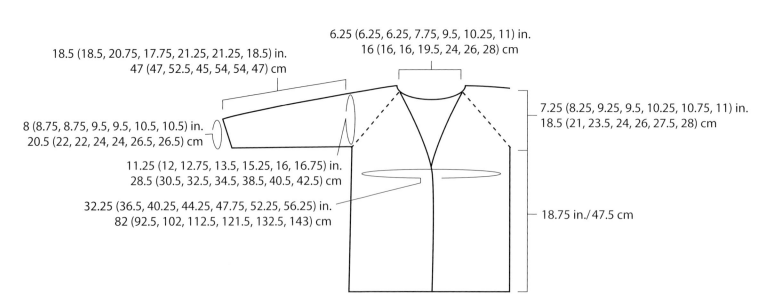

6.25 (6.25, 6.25, 7.75, 9.5, 10.25, 11) in.
16 (16, 16, 19.5, 24, 26, 28) cm

18.5 (18.5, 20.75, 17.75, 21.25, 21.25, 18.5) in.
47 (47, 52.5, 45, 54, 54, 47) cm

7.25 (8.25, 9.25, 9.5, 10.25, 10.75, 11) in.
18.5 (21, 23.5, 24, 26, 27.5, 28) cm

8 (8.75, 8.75, 9.5, 9.5, 10.5, 10.5) in.
20.5 (22, 22, 24, 24, 26.5, 26.5) cm

11.25 (12, 12.75, 13.5, 15.25, 16, 16.75) in.
28.5 (30.5, 32.5, 34.5, 38.5, 40.5, 42.5) cm

32.25 (36.5, 40.25, 44.25, 47.75, 52.25, 56.25) in.
82 (92.5, 102, 112.5, 121.5, 132.5, 143) cm

18.75 in./47.5 cm

Row 28: Knit to end, slipping all sl sts from the previous row.

Rows 29–36: Rep Rows 3–4, then work Rows 1–6 once more.

Row 37: K1, M1, sl 1, *k3, sl 1; rep from * to 2 sts before next m, kfb, k1, (sm, kfb, k1, sl 1, *k3, sl 1; rep from * to 2 sts before next m, kfb, k1) 3 times, sm, kfb, k1, sl 1, *k3, sl 1; rep from * to last st, M1, k1—10 sts inc'd.

Row 38: Knit to end, slipping all sl sts from the previous row.

Rows 39–46: Rep Rows 3–4, then work Rows 1–6 once more.

Row 47: K1, M1, *k3, sl 1; rep from * to 3 sts before next m, k1, kfb, k1, (sm, kfb, k2, sl 1, *k3, sl 1; rep from * to 3 sts before next m, k1, kfb, k1) 3 times, sm, kfb, k2, sl 1, *k3, sl 1; rep from * to last 4 sts, k3, M1, k1—10 sts inc'd.

Row 48: Knit to end, slipping all sl sts from the previous row.

Rows 49–56: Rep Rows 3–4, then work Rows 1–6 once more.

Row 57: K1, M1, k2, sl 1, *k3, sl 1; rep from * to 4 sts before next m, k2, kfb, k1, (sm, kfb, *k3, sl 1; rep from * to 4 sts before next m, k2, kfb, k1) 3 times, sm, kfb, *k3, sl 1; rep from * to last 3 sts, k2, M1, k1—10 sts inc'd.

Row 58: Knit to end, slipping all sl sts from the previous row.

Rows 59–64: Rep Rows 3–4, then work Rows 1–4 once more.

RAGLAN PHASE TWO

Raglan Phase Two has raglan increases only.

Work 20 (14, 16, 10, 6, 0, 0) rows of Raglan Phase Two, as listed below based upon the size worked, and then move on to Raglan Phase Three—261 (283, 291, 321, 359, 385, 389) sts; 37 (42, 43, 48, 54, 59, 59) sts for each front, 53 (57, 59, 63, 69, 73, 73) sts for each sleeve, and 81 (85, 87, 99, 113, 121, 125) sts for the back.

Row 1 (RS): Knit to 2 sts before next m, kfb, k1, (sm, kfb, knit to 2 sts before next m, kfb, k1) 3 times, sm, kfb, knit to end—8 sts inc'd.

Row 2 (WS): K1, purl to last st, k1.

Size 32 Only

Row 3: K2, sl 1, *k3, sl 1; rep from * to 5 sts before next m, k3, kfb, k1, (sm, kfb, sl 1, *k3, sl 1; rep from * to 5 sts before next m, k3, kfb, k1) 3 times, sm, kfb, sl 1, *k3, sl 1; rep from * to last 2 sts, k2—8 sts inc'd.

Sizes 36 (40) Only

Row 3: K1, sl 1, *k3, sl 1; rep from * to 2 sts before next m, kfb, k1, (sm, kfb, k1, sl 1, *k3, sl 1; rep from * to 2 sts before next m, kfb, k1) 3 times, sm, kfb, k1, sl 1, *k3, sl 1; rep from * to last st, k1—8 sts inc'd.

Size 44 Only

Row 3: K1, *k3, sl 1; rep from * to 3 sts before next m, k1, kfb, k1, (sm, kfb, k2, sl 1, *k3, sl 1; rep from * to 3 sts before next m, k1, kfb, k1) 3 times, sm, kfb, k2, sl 1, *k3, sl 1; rep from * to last 4 sts, 4—8 sts inc'd.

Size 48 Only

Row 3: *K3, sl 1; rep from * to 4 sts before next m, k2, kfb, k1, (sm, kfb, *k3, sl 1; rep from * to 4 sts before next m, k2, kfb, k1) 3 times, sm, kfb, *k3, sl 1; rep form * to last 3 sts, k3—8 sts inc'd.

Sizes 32 (36, 40, 44, 48) Only

Row 4: Knit to end, slipping all slip sts from the previous row.

Rows 5-12 (5-12, 5-12, 5-10, 5-6): Rep Rows 1-2 four (four, four, three, one) time(s).

Size 32 Only

Row 13: K1, sl 1, *k3, sl 1; rep from * to 2 sts before next m, kfb, k1, (sm, kfb, k1, sl 1, *k3, sl 1; rep from * to 2 sts before next m, kfb, k1) 3 times, sm, kfb, k1, sl 1, *k3, sl 1; rep from * to last st, k1—8 sts inc'd.

Sizes 36 (40) Only

Row 13: K1, *k3, sl 1; rep from * to 3 sts before next m, k1, kfb, k1, (sm, kfb, k2, sl 1, *k3, sl 1; rep from * to 3 sts before next m, k1, kfb, k1) 3 times, sm, kfb, k2, sl 1, *k3, sl 1; rep from * to last 4 sts, k4—8 sts inc'd.

Sizes 32 (36, 40) Only

Row 14: Knit to end, slipping all slip sts from the previous row.

Sizes 32 (40)

Rows 15-20 (15-16): Rep Rows 1-2 three (one) time(s).

RAGLAN PHASE THREE

Raglan Phase Three has raglan increases on the fronts and back only, no raglan increases on the sleeves.

Beg on Row -- (5, 1, 1, 7, 5, 1), work -- (2, 8, 6, 4, 4, 6) rows of Raglan Phase Three, as listed below for the size worked—261 (287, 307, 333, 367, 393, 401) sts; 37 (43, 48, 51, 56, 61, 62) sts for each front, 53 (57, 59, 63, 69, 73, 73) sts for each sleeve, and 81 (87, 95, 105, 117, 125, 131) sts for the back.

Row 1 (RS): Knit to 2 sts before next m, kfb, k1, sm, knit to next m, sm, kfb, knit to 2 sts before next m, kfb, k1, sm, knit to next m, sm, kfb, knit to end—4 sts inc'd.

Row 2 (WS): K1, purl to last st, k1.

Sizes 40 (44) Only

Row 3: *K3, sl 1; rep from * to 4 sts before next m, k2, kfb, k1, sm, k1, *k3, sl 1; rep from * to 4 sts before next m, k4, sm, kfb, *k3, sl 1; rep from * to 4 sts before next m, k2, kfb, k1, sm, k1 *k3, sl 1; rep from * to 4 sts before next m, k4, sm, kfb, *k3, sl 1; rep from * to last 3 sts, k3—4 sts inc'd.

Size 56 Only

Row 3: *K3, sl 1; rep from * to 5 sts before next m, k3, kfb, k1, sm, k1, sl 1, *k3, sl 1; rep from * to 1 st before next m, k1, sm, kfb, sl 1, *k3, sl 1; rep from * to 5 sts before next m, k3, kfb, k1, sm, k1, sl 1, *k3, sl 1; rep from * to 1 st before next m, k1, sm, kfb, sl 1, *k3, sl 1; rep from * to last 3 sts, k3—4 sts inc'd.

Sizes 40 (44, 56)

Row 4: Knit to end, slipping all sl sts from the previous row.

Sizes 36 (40, 44, 48, 52, 56)

Row 5-6 (5-8, 5-6, 5-10, 5-8, 5-6): Rep Rows 1-2.

DIVIDE BODY AND SLEEVES

Knit to first m, remove m, sl next 53 (57, 59, 63, 69, 73, 73) sts to waste yarn or st holder for sleeve, remove m, CO 3 (5, 5, 7, 5, 7, 13) sts, knit to next m, remove m, slip next 53 (57, 59, 63, 69, 73, 73) sts to waste yarn or st holder for sleeve, remove m, CO 3 (5, 5, 7, 5, 7, 13) sts, knit to end—161 (183, 201, 221, 239, 261, 281) body sts.

BODY

Beg on Row 1 (7, 5, 7, 1, 5, 7) work in the Plain Body Pattern for 12 in. / 30.5 cm or to desired length, ending on Row 10. *Note:* The colored stripes and the ribbing will add approximately 6.75 in. / 17 cm of additional body length.

PLAIN BODY PATTERN

Row 1 (RS): Knit.
Row 2 (WS): K1, purl to last st, k1.
Row 3: K2 (1, 1, 4, 3, 2, 2), *sl 1, k3; rep from * to last 3 (2, 2, 5, 4, 3, 3) sts, sl 1, k2 (1, 1, 4, 3, 2, 2).
Row 4: Knit to end, slipping all sl sts from the previous row.
Rows 5–10: Rep Rows 1–2.

Work 35 rows of the Striped Body Pattern, ending with Row 9. *Note:* The Striped Body is worked in 3 colors, with twice as much of CC1 being used as CC2.

STRIPED BODY PATTERN

Row 1 (RS): With CC1, k4 (3, 3, 2, 1, 4, 4), *sl 1, k3; rep from * to last 5 (4, 4, 3, 2, 5, 5) sts, sl 1, k4 (3, 3, 2, 1, 4, 4).
Row 2 (WS): With CC1, purl to last st, slipping all sl sts from the previous row, end k1.
Row 3: With CC2, k2 (1, 1, 4, 3, 2, 2), *sl 1, k3; rep from * to last 3 (2, 2, 5, 4, 3, 3) sts, sl 1, k2 (1, 1, 4, 3, 2, 2).
Row 4: With CC2, k2 (1, 1, 4, 3, 2, 2), *sl 1, k3; rep from * to last 3 (2, 2, 5, 4, 3, 3) sts, sl 1, k2 (1, 1, 4, 3, 2, 2).
Rows 5–6: Rep Rows 1–2.
Row 7: With MC, k2 (1, 1, 4, 3, 2, 2), *sl 1, k3; rep from * to last 3 (2, 2, 5, 4, 3, 3) sts, sl 1, k2 (1, 1, 4, 3, 2, 2).
Row 8: With MC, k1, purl to last st, slipping all sl sts from the previous row, end k1.
Row 9: With MC, knit.
Row 10: With MC, K1, purl to last st, k1.
Rows 11–12: Rep Rows 9–10.

BOTTOM RIBBING

The Bottom Ribbing is worked in MC.
Setup Row (WS): K1, M1 0 (1, 0, 0, 1, 0, 0) time(s), purl to last st, M1 0 (1, 0, 0, 1, 0, 0) times, k1—161 (185, 201, 221, 241, 261, 281) sts.
Row 1 (RS): (Sl 1, k1) twice *p1, k1, sl 1, k1; rep from * to last st, k1.

Row 2 (WS): Sl 1, *p3, k1; rep from * to end of row.
Row 3: Sl 1, * sl 1, k1, yo, k1, pass sl st over "k1, yo, k1," p1; rep from * to last 4 sts, sl 1, k1, yo, k1, pass sl st over "k1, yo, k1," k1.
Row 4: Sl 1, *p1, sl 1, p1, k1; rep from * to end.
Rep last 4 rows 3 more times, then work rows 1–3 once more.
BO all sts loosely.

SLEEVES

Note: Sleeves are worked in the round. Use your favorite small circumference knitting needles and method.

Place 53 (57, 59, 63, 69, 73, 73) sts back on the needles. CO 1 (1, 2, 2, 3, 3, 5) sts, pm, CO 2 (2, 3, 3, 4, 4, 6) sts, join for knitting in the rnd—56 (60, 64, 68, 76, 80, 84) sts. Knit to m.

Work 11.5 (11.75, 12, 12.25, 12.5, 12.75, 13) in. / 29 (30, 30.5, 31, 32, 32.5, 33) cm in Plain Sleeve Pattern, ending with Rnd 8, and, **AT THE SAME TIME,** work the Dec Rnd every 8th (8th, 8th, 6th, 6th, 6th, 4th) rnd 8 (8, 10, 10, 14, 14, 16) times and keep sl sts lined up in pattern—40 (44, 44, 48, 48, 52, 52) sts. The colored stripes and the ribbing will add approximately 5.5 in. / 14 cm of additional sleeve length. *Note:* The Plain Sleeve Pattern is written for multiples of 4 sts. Make sure to keep the sl sts aligned and in patt as you cont decreasing.

PLAIN SLEEVE PATTERN

Rnd 1: K0 (0, 0, 2, 2, 0, 0), *sl 1, k3; rep from * to last 0 (0, 0, 1, 1, 0, 0) sts, knit to end.
Rnd 2: Purl, slipping all sl sts from the previous rnd.
Rnds 3–10: Knit.
Dec Rnd: K2tog, work in patt to last 3 sts, ssk, k1—2 sts dec'd.
Work Rnds 1–8 of the Plain Sleeve Pattern as established once more.
Work 24 rnds of the Striped Sleeve Pattern.

STRIPED SLEEVE PATTERN

Rnds 1–2: With CC1, k2 (0, 0, 2, 2, 0, 0), *sl 1, k3; rep from * to last 1 (0, 0, 1, 1, 0, 0) sts, knit to end.
Rnd 3: With CC2, k0 (2, 2, 0, 0, 2, 2), *sl 1, k3; rep from * to last 0 (1, 1, 0, 0, 1, 1) sts, knit to end.
Rnd 4: With CC2, purl, slipping all sl sts from the previous rnd.

Rnds 5–6: Rep Rnds 1–2.

Rnds 7–8: With CC1, K0 (2, 2, 0, 0, 2, 2), *sl 1, k3; rep from * to last 0 (1, 1, 0, 0, 1, 1) sts, knit to end.

Rnds 9–12: Knit.

SLEEVE RIBBING

The Sleeve Ribbing is worked in MC.

Setup Rnd: K1, *p1, k3; rep from * to last 3 sts, p1, k2, remove beg of rnd m, k1, replace m, new beg of rnd.

Rnd 1: *P1, sl 1, k1, yo, k1, pass sl st over "k1, yo, k1"; rep from * to end of rnd.

Rnds 2–3: *P1, k1, sl 1, k1; rep from * to end of rnd.

Rnd 4: *P1, k3; rep from * to end of rnd.

Rep last 4 rnds 3 more times, then work Rnd 1 once more.

BO all sts loosely.

Rep for second sleeve.

FINISHING

FRONT BANDS AND COLLAR

With RS facing, MC, and beg at bottom of right front, pick up and knit approximately 3 sts for every 4 rows of knitting up to neck CO, and then pick up and knit 1 st for each CO st around neck, then 3 sts for every 4 rows of knitting along left front edge. The exact number of sts here isn't important, but the ribbing needs to be a multiple of 4 sts plus 1, so decrease away a few sts if necessary in the first row to reach that multiple.

FRONT RIBBING

Setup Row (WS): Sl 1, *p3, k1; rep from * to end of row.

Row 1 (RS): Sl 1, *sl 1, k1, yo, k1, pass sl st over "k1, yo, k1," p1; rep from * to last 4 sts, sl 1, k1, yo, k1, pass sl st over "k1, yo, k1," k1.

Row 2 (WS): Sl 1, *p1, sl 1, p1, k1; rep from * to end.

Row 3: (Sl 1, k1) twice, *p1, k1, sl 1, k1; rep from * to last st, k1.

Row 4: Sl 1, *p3, k1; rep from * to end of row.

Rep last 4 rows three more times, then work Row 1 once more.

BO all sts loosely.

Seam up underarms. Weave in all ends. Block lightly to schematic measurements.

Shanna

The swirling rib on Shanna will keep you cozy all winter long.
Worked up in bulky, easy-care yarn, it will be a quick knit
and a classic winter staple for years to come.

SIZE
Bust: 36.25 (40, 44.25, 48, 52.25, 56.5, 60.75) in.
/ 92 (101.5, 112.5, 122, 132.5, 143.5, 154.5) cm

YARN
Patons Classic Wool Roving; Bulky weight; 100%
wool; 120 yd. / 110 m; 3.5 oz. / 100 g per ball
  Plum: 6 (7, 8, 9, 10, 12, 13) balls

NEEDLES
US 10 (6.0 mm); adjust needle size as necessary
to achieve gauge.

NOTIONS
- stitch markers
- tapestry needle
- waste yarn or stitch holders

GAUGE
15 sts and 21 rnds = 4 in. / 10 cm in St st

PATTERN STITCHES
2x2 Rib
  Rnd 1: *K2, p2; rep from * to end of rnd.
  Rep Rnd 1 for patt.
St st in the Rnd
  Rnd 1: Knit.
  Rep Rnd 1 for patt.

INSTRUCTIONS

NECK

CO 56 (60, 68, 72, 76, 80, 84) sts. Pm and join to work in the rnd, being careful not to twist sts. Work in 2x2 Rib for 13 (13, 14, 14, 16, 16, 16) rnds. Neck measures approximately 2.5 (2.5, 2.75, 2.75, 3, 3, 3) in. / 6.5 (6.5, 7, 7, 7.5, 7.5, 7.5) cm.

YOKE

Rnd 1: *K1, M1, k1, M1, p2; rep from * to end of rnd—84 (90, 102, 108, 114, 120, 126) sts.

Rnds 2–4: *K4, p2; rep from * to end of rnd.

Rnds 5–8: *K2, p2, k2; rep from * to end of rnd.

Rnd 9: *P2, k1, M1, k2, M1, k1; rep from * to end of rnd—112 (120, 136, 144, 152, 160, 168) sts.

Rnds 10–12: *P2, k6; rep from * to end of rnd.

Rnds 13–16: *K6, p2; rep from * to end of rnd.

Rnd 17: *K3, M1, k1, p2, k1, M1, k1; rep from * to end of rnd—140 (150, 170, 180, 190, 200, 210) sts.

Rnds 18–20: *K5, p2, k3; rep from * to end of rnd.

Rnds 21–24: *K3, p2, k5; rep from * to end of rnd.

Rnd 25: *M1, k1, p2, k6, M1, k1; rep from * to end of rnd—168 (180, 204, 216, 240, 252) sts.

Rnds 26–28: *K2, p2, k8; rep from * to end of rnd.

Rnds 29–32: *P2, k10; rep from * to end of rnd.

Rnd 33: *K1, M1, k8, M1, k1, p2; rep from * to end of rnd—196 (210, 238, 252, 266, 280, 294) sts.

Rnds 34–36: *K12, p2; rep from * to end of rnd.

Rnds 37–40: *K10, p2, k2; rep from * to end of rnd.

Sizes 52.25 (56.5, 60.75) Only

Rnd 41: *K7, M1, k1, p2, k1, M1, k3; rep from * to end of rnd—304 (320, 336) sts.

Rnds 42–44: *K9, p2, k5; rep from * to end of rnd.

All Sizes

Work in St st in the rnd for 3 (8, 11, 13, 13, 16, 18) more rows or until yoke measures approximately 8 (9, 9.5, 10, 11, 11.5, 12) in. / 20.5 (23, 24, 25.5, 28, 29, 30.5) cm from Rnd 1.

DIVIDE BODY AND SLEEVES

Next Rnd: *K59 (64, 73, 78, 93, 99, 105), place next 39 (41, 46, 48, 59, 61, 63) sts on waste yarn or st holder for sleeve, CO 9 (11, 10, 12, 5, 7, 9) sts for underarm; rep from * once—136 (150, 166, 180, 196, 212, 228) sts remain for body.

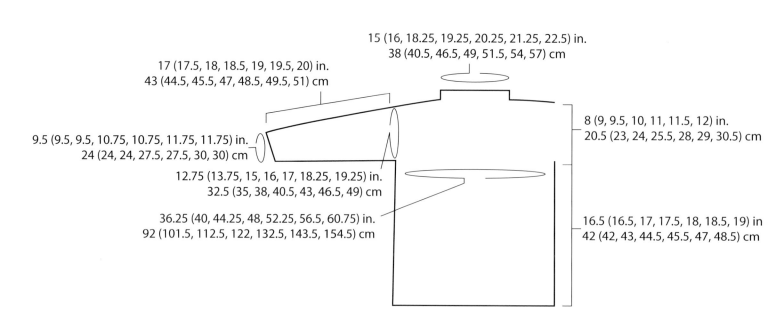

15 (16, 18.25, 19.25, 20.25, 21.25, 22.5) in.
38 (40.5, 46.5, 49, 51.5, 54, 57) cm

17 (17.5, 18, 18.5, 19, 19.5, 20) in.
43 (44.5, 45.5, 47, 48.5, 49.5, 51) cm

8 (9, 9.5, 10, 11, 11.5, 12) in.
20.5 (23, 24, 25.5, 28, 29, 30.5) cm

9.5 (9.5, 9.5, 10.75, 10.75, 11.75, 11.75) in.
24 (24, 24, 27.5, 27.5, 30, 30) cm

12.75 (13.75, 15, 16, 17, 18.25, 19.25) in.
32.5 (35, 38, 40.5, 43, 46.5, 49) cm

36.25 (40, 44.25, 48, 52.25, 56.5, 60.75) in.
92 (101.5, 112.5, 122, 132.5, 143.5, 154.5) cm

16.5 (16.5, 17, 17.5, 18, 18.5, 19) in
42 (42, 43, 44.5, 45.5, 47, 48.5) cm

BODY

Work St st in the rnd for 74 (74, 75, 77, 79, 81, 84) rnds. Body measures approximately 14 (14, 14.25, 14.75, 15, 15.5, 16) in. / 35.5 (35.5, 36, 37.5, 38, 39.5, 40.5) cm.

Sizes 40 (44.25) Only
Dec Rnd: K1, k2tog, k72 (80), k2tog, knit to end—148 (164) sts.

RIBBED HEM

Work in 2x2 Rib for 13 (13, 14, 14, 16, 16, 16) rnds. Ribbing measures approximately 2.5 (2.5, 2.75, 2.75, 3, 3, 3) in. / 6.5 (6.5, 7, 7, 7.5, 7.5, 7.5) cm. BO all sts loosely in patt.

SLEEVES

Note: Sleeves are worked in the round. Use your favorite small circumference knitting needles and method.

   Place 39 (41, 46, 48, 59, 61, 63) held sleeve sts back on the needles to work in the rnd. CO 5 (6, 5, 6, 3, 4, 5) sts, pm for beg of rnd, cast on 4 (5, 5, 6, 2, 3, 4) sts, join for knitting in the rnd—48 (52, 56, 60, 64, 68, 72) sts. Knit to m.

   Work in St st in the Rnd for 10 (8, 8, 8, 6, 6, 6) rnds. Sleeve measures approximately 2 (1.5, 1.5, 1.5, 1.25, 1.25, 1.25) in. / 5 (4, 4, 4, 3, 3, 3) cm.

Dec Rnd: K1, k2tog, knit to last 3 sts, ssk, k1—2 sts dec.

Rep Dec Rnd every 10 (8, 8, 8, 6, 6, 6) rnds 5 (7, 9, 9, 11, 11, 13) times more—36 (36, 36, 40, 40, 44, 44) sts.

Continue in St st in the rnd until sleeve measures 15 (15.5, 16, 16.5, 17, 17.5, 18) in. / 38 (39.5, 40.5, 42, 43, 44.5, 45.5) cm.

Work 2x2 Rib for 2 in. / 5 cm.

BO all sts loosely in patt.

Rep for second sleeve.

FINISHING

Seam up underarms. Weave in all ends. Block lightly to schematic measurements.

Beryl

Squishy hand-dyed yarn and simple ribs and slip stitches make this yoke sweater an easy-breezy wardrobe staple. Want to make it extra cozy? Sew in a zipper along the i-cord front edges to make this comfy cardigan a jacket you won't want to take off!

SIZE
Bust: 31 (34.75, 36, 41.25, 49.25, 52.5, 54.75) in. / 78.5 (88.5, 91.5, 105, 125, 133.5, 139) cm

YARN
Fiber Seed Sprout Worsted; Worsted weight; 90% merino wool, 10% nylon; 250 yd. / 230 m, 4.8 oz. / 136 g per skein
Boca: 4 (5, 6, 7, 8, 9, 9) skeins

NEEDLES
US 7 (4.5 mm); adjust needle size as necessary to achieve gauge.

NOTIONS
- stitch markers
- tapestry needle
- waste yarn or stitch holders

GAUGE
18 sts and 24 rows = 4 in. / 10 cm in blocked St st

PATTERN STITCHES
St st Flat
  Row 1 (RS): Knit.
  Row 2 (WS): Purl.
  Rep Rows 1–2 for patt.
Rev St st Flat
  Row 1 (RS): Purl.
  Row 2 (WS): Knit.
  Rep Rows 1–2 for patt.
St st in the Rnd
  Rnd 1: Knit.
  Rep Rnd 1 for patt.
Rev St st in the Rnd
  Rnd 1: Purl.
  Rep Rnd 1 for patt.

NOTES

In the Slip Rib Pattern instructions, you are instructed to "knit the 2 sl strands tog with the next st." This means you will lift the strands created by slipped stitches on previous rows up onto the left needle from front to back and then knit them together with the next stitch on the needle. No stitches are decreased.

INSTRUCTIONS

COLLAR

CO 66 (66, 70, 70, 74, 74, 78) sts, but do not join.
Row 1 (RS): K2, *p2, k2; rep from * to end.
Row 2 (WS): P2, *k2, p2; rep from * to end.
Rows 3–10: Rep Rows 1–2.
Row 11: Rep Row 1.
Row 12: P1, knit to last st, p1.

YOKE

Work 1 (1, 2, 2, 2, 2, 2) reps of the 28-row Slip Rib Pattern that follows, incorporating the Inc Row as directed on Rows 1 and 19.

Sizes 31 (34.75, 49.25, 52.5, 54.75) Only
Work Rows 1–20 (20, 2, 2, 2) once more, incorporating the Inc Row as directed on Rows 1 and 19.

SLIP RIB PATTERN

Row 1 (RS): Work next Inc Row as directed on page 21 for each repeat.
Row 2 (WS): P1, knit to last st, p1.
Row 3: K1, p1, *k2, p2; rep from * to last 4 sts, k2, p1, k1.
Row 4: P1, k1, p2, *k2, p2; rep from * to last 2 sts, k1, p1.
Row 5: K1, p1, sl 2 wyif, *p2, sl 2 wyif; rep from * to last 2 sts, p1, k1.
Row 6: P1, k1, sl 2 wyib, *k2, sl 2 wyib; rep from * to last 2 sts, k1, p1.
Rows 7–8: Rep Rows 3–4.
Row 9: K1, p1, knit the 2 sl strands tog with next st (see Notes), k1, *p2, knit the 2 sl strands tog with next st, k1; rep from * to last 2 sts, p1, k1.
Row 10: P1, k1, p2, *k2, p2; rep from * to last 2 sts, k1, p1.
Rows 11–12: Rep Rows 5–6.
Rows 13–14: Rep Rows 3–4.
Row 15: K1, p1, k1, knit the 2 sl strands tog with next st, *p2, k1, knit the 2 sl strands tog with next st; rep from * to last 2 sts, p1, k1.
Row 16: P1, k1, p2, *k2, p2; rep from * to last 2 sts, k1, p1.
Row 17: K1, p1, k2, *p2, k2; rep from * to last 2 sts, p1, k1.
Row 18: P1, knit to last 2 sts, k1, p1.
Row 19: Work next Inc Row as directed on page 21 for each repeat.
Row 20: P1, knit to last 2 sts, k1, p1.
Row 21: K2, *p2, k2; rep from * to end.
Row 22: P2, *k2, p2; rep from * to end.

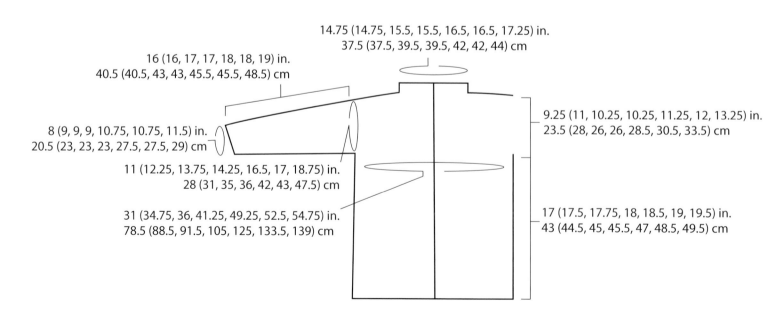

14.75 (14.75, 15.5, 15.5, 16.5, 16.5, 17.25) in.
37.5 (37.5, 39.5, 39.5, 42, 42, 44) cm

16 (16, 17, 17, 18, 18, 19) in.
40.5 (40.5, 43, 43, 45.5, 45.5, 48.5) cm

8 (9, 9, 9, 10.75, 10.75, 11.5) in.
20.5 (23, 23, 23, 27.5, 27.5, 29) cm

11 (12.25, 13.75, 14.25, 16.5, 17, 18.75) in.
28 (31, 35, 36, 42, 43, 47.5) cm

31 (34.75, 36, 41.25, 49.25, 52.5, 54.75) in.
78.5 (88.5, 91.5, 105, 125, 133.5, 139) cm

9.25 (11, 10.25, 10.25, 11.25, 12, 13.25) in.
23.5 (28, 26, 26, 28.5, 30.5, 33.5) cm

17 (17.5, 17.75, 18, 18.5, 19, 19.5) in.
43 (44.5, 45, 45.5, 47, 48.5, 49.5) cm

Rows 23–27: Cont in Rib as established.

Row 28: P1, knit to last 2 sts, k1, p1.

Inc Row 1 (First Rep): K1, p13 (11, 13, 11, 11, 9, 9), M1 (*p1, M1; rep from * to last 14 (12, 14, 12, 12, 10, 10) sts, purl to last st, M1, k1—106 (110, 114, 118, 126, 130, 138) sts.

Inc Row 19 (First Rep): K1, p4 (4, 1, 2, 2, 4, 6), M1 0 (1, 1, 1, 0, 1, 1) time(s), *p2, M1; rep from * to last 5 (5, 2, 3, 3, 5, 7) sts, purl to last st, M1 0 (1, 0, 1, 0, 1, 1) time(s), k1—154 (162, 170, 176, 186, 192, 202) sts.

Inc Row 1 (Second Rep): K1, p6 (4, 3, 3, 2, 3, 4), M1 0 (0, 1, 1, 1, 1, 0) time(s), *p4 (3, 3, 2, 2, 2, 2), M1; rep from * to last 7 (4, 4, 4, 3, 4, 5) sts, purl to last st, M1 1 (1, 1, 1, 1, 1, 0) time(s), k1—190 (214, 226, 262, 278, 286, 298) sts.

Inc Row 19 (Second Rep): K1, p4 (4, 4, 6, 2, 4, 4), M1 1 (1, 0, 1, 1, 1, 0) time(s), *p6 (6, 6, 8, 8, 6, 6), M1; rep from * to last 5 (5, 5, 7, 3, 5, 5) sts, purl to last st, M1 1 (1, 0, 0, 1, 1, 0) time(s), k1—222 (250, 262, 294, 314, 334, 346) sts.

Sizes 49.25 (52.5, 54.75) Only

Inc Row 1 (Third Rep): K1, p12 (12, 10), M1 0 (1, 1) time(s), *p12 (14, 12), M1; rep from * to last 13 (13, 11) sts, purl to last st, M1 0, (1, 0) time(s) k1—338 (358, 374) sts.

All Sizes

222 (250, 262, 294, 338, 358, 374) sts.

Row 1 (RS): Knit.

Row 2 (WS): K1, purl to last st, k1.

Rep the last 2 rows 2 (3, 0, 0, 1, 2, 4) times.

DIVIDE BODY AND SLEEVES

Note: When dividing the body and sleeves, sizes 40 and 44 are done in reverse stockinette to finish the patterning, whereas all other sizes are done in regular stockinette.

Sizes 31 (36, 49.25, 52.5, 54.75)

Dividing Row (RS): K33 (37, 52, 55, 56), place 45 (51, 66, 69, 74) sts on waste yarn or st holder for sleeve, CO 4 (4, 8, 8, 10) sts, k66 (74, 102,

110, 114), place 45 (51, 66, 69, 74) sts on waste yarn or st holder for sleeve, CO 4 (4, 8, 8, 10) sts, knit to end—140 (156, 222, 236, 246) sts.
Next Row (WS): Purl.

Sizes 36 (41.25) Only
Dividing Row (RS): K1, p37 (42), place 56 (58) sts on waste yarn or st holder for sleeve, CO 6 sts, p76 (86), place 56 (58) sts on waste yarn or st holder for sleeve, CO 6 sts, purl to last st, k1—162 (186) sts.
Next Row (WS): P1, knit to last st, p1.

BODY

Work in St st Flat until body measures 15 (15.5, 15.75, 16, 16.5, 17, 17.5) in. / 38 (39.5, 40, 40.5, 42, 43, 44.5) cm, or 2 in. / 5 cm less than desired length. Work bottom ribbing as follows.

RIBBING HEM
Row 1 (RS): K2, *p2, k2; rep from * to end.
Row 2 (WS): P2, *k2, p2; rep from * to end.
Rows 3–10: Rep Rows 1–2.
Row 11: Rep Row 1.
Row 12: P1, knit to last st, p1.
BO all sts loosely in patt.

SLEEVES

Note: Sleeves are worked in the round. Use your favorite small circumference knitting needles and method.
   Place 45 (51, 56, 58, 66, 69, 74) held sleeve sts back on needles to work in the rnd. CO 2 (2, 3, 3, 4, 4, 5) sts, pm for beg of rnd, CO 2 (2, 3, 3, 4, 4, 5) sts—49 (55, 62, 64, 74, 77, 84) sts.

Sizes 36 (41.25) Only
Work Rev St st in the Rnd for 2 rnds.

All Sizes
Work St st in the Rnd until Sleeve measures 2 in. / 5 cm from underarm.
Dec Rnd: K1, k2tog, knit to last 3 sts, ssk, k1—2 sts dec'd.
Rep Dec Rnd every 12 (10, 6, 6, 6, 6, 5)th rnd 5 (7, 11, 12, 13, 14, 15) times—37 (39, 38, 38, 46, 47, 52) sts. Work until sleeve measures 14 (14, 15, 15, 16, 16, 17) in. / 35.5 (35.5, 38, 38, 40.5, 40.5, 43) cm, or 2 in. / 5 cm less than desired length.

Next Rnd: K1, k2tog 1 (0, 0, 0, 0, 0, 0) time, M1 0 (1, 1, 1, 1, 1, 0) time, knit to last st, M1 0 (0, 1, 1, 1, 0, 0) time, k1—36 (40, 40, 40, 48, 48, 52) sts.
Ribbing Rnd: *K2, p2; rep from * to end.
Rep last rnd 11 times.
BO all sts loosely.

FINISHING

RIGHT FRONT BAND
With RS facing and beg at lower Right Front edge and working toward collar, pick up and knit 3 sts for every 4 rows along Right Front. Using the cable or knitted method, CO 3 sts. Work i-cord BO as follows:
Row 1 (RS): K2, ssk. Move sts to other end of needles to prepare for working a RS row again. Rep Row 1 until all sts are bound off and only 3 sts remain. BO all sts.

LEFT FRONT BAND
With RS facing and beg at collar and working down Left Front edge, pick up and knit 3 sts for every 4 rows along Left Front. Using the cable or knitted method, CO 3 sts. Work i-cord BO.

   Sew up underarm seams. Weave in all ends. Block lightly to schematic measurements.

Rhoda

The stylish collar on Rhoda makes it an easy sweater to dress up or down. The flattering wide ribs make this simple sweater just a little bit more than it appears.

SIZE
Bust: 32.75 (37.5, 40.75, 45.5, 48.75, 53.5, 56.75) in. / 83 (95.5, 103.5, 115.5, 124, 136, 144) cm

YARN
Berroco Fiora; DK weight; 40% cotton, 30% rayon/viscose, 15% alpaca, 10% nylon, and 5% wool; 246 yd. / 225 m, 3.5 oz. / 100 g per skein
  Augusta: 6 (7, 8, 9, 10, 11, 12) skeins

NEEDLES
US 5 (3.75 mm); adjust needle size as necessary to achieve gauge.

NOTIONS
- stitch markers
- tapestry needle
- waste yarn or stitch holders

GAUGE
20 sts and 28 rows = 4 in. / 10 cm in St st

PATTERN STITCHES
Zigzag Pattern (also charted on page 27)
  Row 1 (RS): *K2, p2, k2, p5; rep from *.
  Row 2 (WS): *K5, p2, k2, p2; rep from *.
  Row 3: *K2, p2, k5, p2; rep from *.
  Row 4: *k2, p5, k2, p2; rep from *.
  Row 5: *K2, p5, k2, p2; rep from *.
  Row 6: *K2, p2, k5, p2; rep from *.
  Row 7: *K5, p2, k2, p2; rep from *.
  Row 8: *K2, p2, k2, p5; rep from *.
  Row 9: *P3, (k2, p2) twice; rep from *.
  Row 10: *(K2, p2) twice, k3; rep from *.
  Row 11: *K1, p2, k2, p2, k4; rep from *.
  Row 12: *P4, k2, p2, k2, p1; rep from *.
  Row 13: *K1, p2, k2, p5, k1; rep from *.
  Row 14: *P1, k5, p2, k2, p1; rep from *.
  Row 15: *K1, p2, k5, p2, k1; rep from *.
  Row 16: *P1, k2, p5, k2, p1; rep from *.
  Row 17: *K1, p5, k2, p2, k1; rep from *.

Row 18: *P1, k2, p2, k5, p1; rep from *.
Row 19: *K4, p2, k2, p2, k1; rep from *.
Row 20: *P1, k2, p2, k2, p4; rep from *.
Row 21: *(P2, k2) twice, p3; rep from *.
Row 22: *K3, (p2, k2) twice; rep from *.
Row 23: *P2, k2, p2, k5; rep from *.
Row 24: *P5, k2, p2, k2; rep from *.
Row 25: *P2, k2, p5, k2; rep from *.
Row 26: *P2, k5, p2, k2; rep from *.
Row 27: *P2, k5, p2, k2; rep from *.
Row 28: *P2, k2, p5, k2; rep from *.
Row 29: *P5, k2, p2, k2; rep from *.
Row 30: *P2, k2, p2, k5; rep from *.
Row 31: *K3, (p2, k2) twice; rep from *.
Row 32: *(P2, k2) twice, p3; rep from *.
Row 33: *P1, k2, p2, k2, p4; rep from *.
Row 34: *K4, p2, k2, p2, k1; rep from *.
Row 35: *P1, k2, p2, k5, p1; rep from *.
Row 36: *K1, p5, k2, p2, k1; rep from *.
Row 37: *P1, k2, p5, k2, p1; rep from *.
Row 38: *K1, p2, k5, p2, k1; rep from *.
Row 39: *P1, k5, p2, k2, p1; rep from *.
Row 40: *K1, p2, k2, p5, k1; rep from *.
Row 41: *P4, k2, p2, k2, p1; rep from *.
Row 42: *K1, p2, k2, p2, k4; rep from *.
Row 43: *(K2, p2) twice, k3; rep from *.
Row 44: *P3, (k2, p2) twice); rep from *.
Row 45: *K2, p2, k2, p5; rep from *.
Row 46: *K5, p2, k2, p2; rep from *.
Row 47: *K2, p2, k5, p2; rep from *.
Row 48: *K2, p5, k2, p2; rep from *.

INSTRUCTIONS

COWL

CO 3 sts. Work i-cord CO as follows: *Kfb, k2, sl 3 sts back to LH needle; rep from * 32 more times, kfb, k2—37 sts; 3 for the i-cord, 34 sts for the cowl. The cowl is worked flat as follows:

RS Rows: K3, work 3 reps of the Zigzag Pattern, k1.

WS Rows: K1, work 3 reps of the Zigzag Pattern, sl 3 pwise wyif.

Cont in Zigzag Pattern as established for a total of 116 (116, 120, 120, 124, 124, 132) rows ending with a WS row. BO using an i-cord BO as follows:

Next Row (RS): *K2, ssk, sl 3 sts back to LH needle; rep from * 33 times, k1, ssk, sl 2 sts back to LH needle, ssk—1 st remains.

Turn work and pick up and knit 115 (115, 119, 119, 123, 123, 131) sts along the garter edge—about 3 sts for every 4 rows—116 (116, 120, 120, 124, 124, 132) sts total. *Note:* There will be about 16 rows remaining of the cowl; this portion will hang open in the finished garment.

Note: You will now be working in the rnd. The first m placed is the beg of rnd m. This rnd establishes the 6x2 rib for the sleeves and body.

Setup Rnd: *Pm, k1, kfb, k0 (0, 1, 1, 2, 2, 4), p2, (k6, p2) 5 times, k0 (0, 1, 1, 2, 2, 4), kfb, k1, pm, kfb, p2, k6, p2, kfb; rep from * once more, 8 sts inc'd, 4 m placed—124 (124, 128, 128, 132, 132, 140) sts.

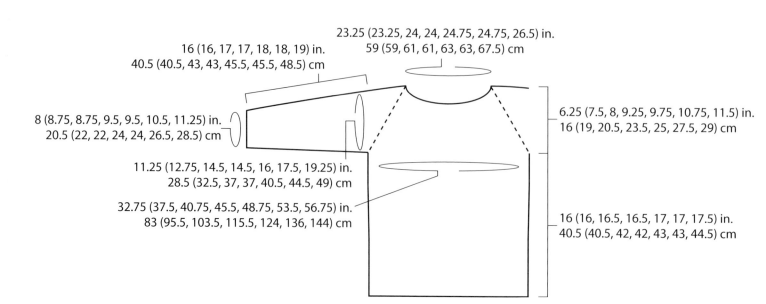

16 (16, 17, 17, 18, 18, 19) in.
40.5 (40.5, 43, 43, 45.5, 45.5, 48.5) cm

23.25 (23.25, 24, 24, 24.75, 24.75, 26.5) in.
59 (59, 61, 61, 63, 63, 67.5) cm

8 (8.75, 8.75, 9.5, 9.5, 10.5, 11.25) in.
20.5 (22, 22, 24, 24, 26.5, 28.5) cm

6.25 (7.5, 8, 9.25, 9.75, 10.75, 11.5) in.
16 (19, 20.5, 23.5, 25, 27.5, 29) cm

11.25 (12.75, 14.5, 14.5, 16, 17.5, 19.25) in.
28.5 (32.5, 37, 37, 40.5, 44.5, 49) cm

32.75 (37.5, 40.75, 45.5, 48.75, 53.5, 56.75) in.
83 (95.5, 103.5, 115.5, 124, 136, 144) cm

16 (16, 16.5, 16.5, 17, 17, 17.5) in.
40.5 (40.5, 42, 42, 43, 43, 44.5) cm

Zigzag Pattern

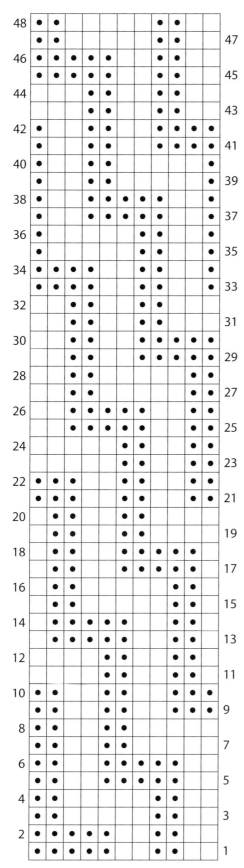

☐ Knit on RS, purl on WS

● Purl on RS, knit on WS

Next Rnd: Work even as established, slipping the markers, knitting the knits, and purling the purls.

YOKE

RAGLAN PHASE A—ALL SIZES

Raglan Phase A has both front/back and sleeve increases.

Work Rnds 1–2 of Raglan Phase A 11 (19, 21, 23, 28, 29, 35) times—212 (276, 296, 312, 356, 364, 420) sts; 70 (86, 92, 96, 108, 110, 126) for each front/back and 36 (52, 56, 60, 70, 72, 84) sts for each sleeve.

Rnd 1: *K1, kfb, work in rib patt as established to 2 sts before next m, kfb, k1, sm, kfb, work in rib patt as established to 1 st before next m, kfb, sm; rep from * once—8 sts inc'd.

Rnd 2: Work in rib patt as established, knitting the knits and purling the purls, making sure to keep the first and last st of the front/back as a knit st.

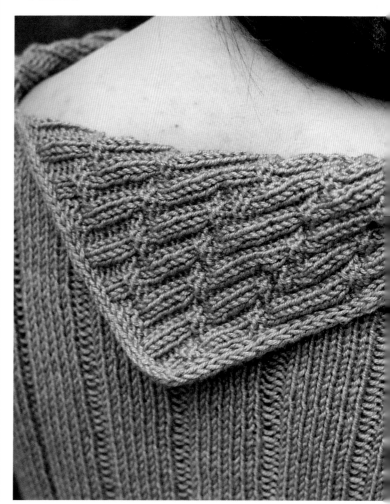

RAGLAN PHASE B–SIZES 32.75 (37.5, 40.75) ONLY

Raglan Phase B has a combination of front/back and sleeve increases.

Work Rnds 1-4 of Raglan Phase B 4 (2, 3) times—260 (300, 332) sts; 78 (90, 98) sts for each front/back and 52 (60, 68) sts for each sleeve.

Rnd 1: *K1, kfb, work in rib patt as established to 2 sts before next m, kfb, k1, sm, kfb, work in rib patt as established to 1 st before next m, kfb, sm; rep from * once—8 sts inc'd.

Rnd 2: Work in rib patt as established, knitting the knits and purling the purls, making sure to keep the first and last st of the front/back as a knit st.

Rnd 3: *K1, work in rib patt as established to 1 st before next m, k1, sm, kfb, work in rib patt as established to 1 st before next m, kfb, sm; rep from * once—4 sts inc'd on sleeves only.

Rnd 4: Rep Rnd 2.

RAGLAN PHASE C–SIZES 45.5 (48.75, 53.5, 56.75) ONLY

Raglan Phase C has a combination of front/back and sleeve increases.

Work Rnds 1-4 of Raglan Phase C 3 (2, 4, 2) times—348 (380, 412, 444) sts; 108 (116, 126, 134) sts for each front/back and 66 (74, 80, 88) sts for each sleeve.

Rnd 1: *K1, kfb, work in rib patt as established to 2 sts before next m, kfb, k1, sm, kfb, work in rib patt as established to 1 st before next m, kfb, sm; rep from * once—8 sts inc'd.

Rnd 2: Work in rib patt as established, knitting the knits and purling the purls, making sure to keep the first and last st of the front/back as a knit st.

Rnd 3: *K1, kfb, work in rib pattern as established to 2 sts before next m, kfb, k1, sm, work in rib patt as established to next m, sm; rep from * once—4 sts inc'd on front/back only.

Rnd 4: Rep Rnd 2.

All Sizes

Work 4 (4, 0, 4, 2, 0, 0) rnds even in patts as established.

DIVIDE BODY AND SLEEVES

Work in rib patt as established to first m, remove m, sl next 52 (60, 68, 66, 74, 80, 88) sleeve sts to waste yarn or st holder, CO 2 (2, 2, 3, 3, 4, 4) sts, pm for side, CO 2 (2, 2, 3, 3, 4, 4) sts, work in rib patt as established to next m, remove m, sl next 52 (60, 68, 66, 74, 80, 88) sleeve sts to waste yarn or st holder, CO 2 (2, 2, 3, 3, 4, 4) sts, place new beg of round m, CO 2 (2, 2, 3, 3, 4, 4) sts, work in rib patt as established to end—164 (188, 204, 228, 244, 268, 284) body sts.

BODY

Work in rib patt as established until body measures 14 (14, 14.5, 14.5, 15, 15, 15.5) in. / 35.5 (35.5, 37, 37, 38, 38, 39.5) cm from underarm or to 2 in. / 5 cm less than desired body length. Switch from k6, p2 rib to a k2, p2 rib and work in k2, p2 rib for 2 in. / 5 cm. BO all sts loosely.

SLEEVES

Note: Sleeves are worked in the round. Use your favorite small circumference knitting needles and method.

Place 52 (60, 68, 66, 74, 80, 88) held sleeve sts back on the needles to work in the rnd. CO 2 (2, 2, 3, 3, 4, 4) sts, pm, CO 2 (2, 2, 3, 3, 4, 4) sts—56 (64, 72, 72, 80, 88, 96) sts. Work in patt to m.

Work 4 rnds in rib patt as established.

Work the following Dec Rnd every 10 (8, 6, 8, 6, 6, 6)th rnd 8 (10, 14, 12, 16, 18, 20) times—40 (44, 44, 48, 48, 52, 56) sts.

Dec Rnd: Work 1 st in patt, k2tog, work in rib patt as established to last 3 sts, ssk, work 1 st in patt—2 sts dec'd.

Continuing in rib patt as established, work until sleeve measures 14 (14, 15, 15, 16, 16, 17) in. / 35.5 (35.5, 38, 38, 40.5, 40.5, 43) cm from underarm or 2 in. / 5 cm less than desired sleeve length. Switch from k6, p2 rib to a k2, p2 rib and work in k2, p2 rib for 2 in. / 5 cm. BO all sts loosely.

Rep for second sleeve.

FINISHING

Sew up underarm seams. Weave in all ends. Block lightly to schematic measurements.

CHAPTER 3

Captivating Colorwork

There are so many gorgeous yarn colors available, why would you ever want to limit yourself to just one? In this chapter we are all about the stripes— plain stripes and stripes with slipped stitches to make the most of these stunning shades. And the best part about colorwork is that you get to choose your favorite hues!

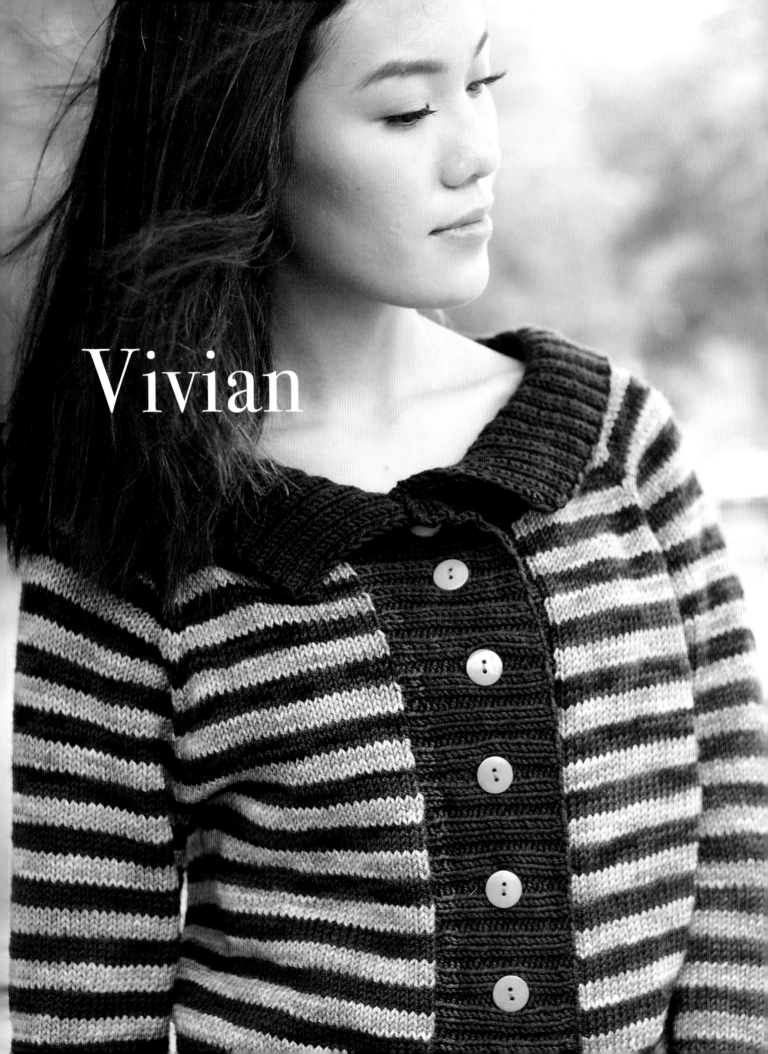

Vivian

Simple stripes are playful and fun when you choose a knock-out contrast color to really bring some punch to your knitting. Throw in bright-colored buttons, and you have a one-of-a-kind sweater made just for you!

SIZE
Bust without bands: 28.75 (32.75, 36.75, 40.75, 44.75, 48.75, 52.75) in. / 73 (83, 93.5, 103.5, 113.5, 124, 134) cm
  Bust with bands buttoned: 31.75 (35.75, 39.75, 43.75, 47.75, 51.75, 55.75) in. / 80.5 (91, 101, 111, 121.5, 131.5, 141.5) cm

YARN
Baah Sonoma; DK weight; 100% merino wool; 234 yd. / 214 m, 3.5 oz. / 100 g per skein
  Night Sky (MC): 3 (4, 5, 5, 6, 6, 7) skeins
  Flamingo Pink (CC): 2 (3, 3, 4, 4, 5, 5) skeins

NEEDLES
US 6 (4.0 mm); adjust needle size as necessary to achieve gauge.

NOTIONS
- stitch markers
- tapestry needle
- waste yarn or stitch holders
- twelve ¾-in. / 1.9-cm buttons

GAUGE
20 sts and 28 rows = 4 in. / 10 cm in St st

PATTERN STITCHES
St st
  Row 1 (RS): Knit.
  Row 2 (WS): K1, purl to last st, k1.
  Rep last 2 rows for patt.

NOTES
Sweater is worked in 4-row stripes, alternating main color (MC) and contrast color (CC).

INSTRUCTIONS

YOKE

With CC, CO 76 (78, 84, 88, 94, 114, 126) sts.

Setup Row (WS): With CC, k1, p10 (11, 13, 14, 16, 19, 22), pm, p10 (9, 8, 8, 7, 11, 11), pm, p34 (36, 40, 42, 46, 52, 58), pm, p10 (9, 8, 8, 7, 11, 11), pm, p10 (11, 13, 14, 16, 19, 22), k1.

Working in St st, keeping the first and last st of every row as a knit st, and alternating colors every 4 rows, work the following Inc Rnd every other rnd 14 (20, 22, 28, 33, 35, 37) times, and then every 4th rnd 6 (4, 4, 2, 0, 0, 0) times—236 (270, 292, 328, 358, 394, 422) sts; 31 (36, 40, 45, 50, 55, 60) sts for each front, 50 (57, 60, 68, 73, 81, 85) sts for each sleeve, 74 (84, 92, 102, 112, 122, 132) sts for the back.

Inc Row (RS): *Knit to 1 st before m, M1, k1, sm, k1, M1; rep from * three times, knit to end—8 sts inc'd.

Next Row (WS): K1, purl to last st, k1.

DIVIDE FOR SLEEVES AND BODY

Next Row (RS): Removing raglan m, knit to m, place next 50 (57, 60, 68, 73, 81, 85) sts on waste yarn or st holder for sleeve, CO 4 (4, 6, 6, 6, 6, 6) sts, knit across back sts, place next 50 (57, 60, 68, 73, 81, 85) sts on waste yarn or st holder for sleeve, CO 4 (4, 6, 6, 6, 6, 6) sts, knit to end—144 (164, 184, 204, 224, 244, 264) sts for body.

BODY

Continue working in St st, keeping the first and last st of every row as a knit st, and alternating colors every 4 rows as established until body measures 15 in. / 38 cm, or 3 in. / 7.5 cm shorter than desired length, ending with 4 rows of CC. Cut CC.

Work 3 in. / 7.5 cm of Ribbing with MC as follows.

RIBBING

Row 1 (RS): K3, *p2, k2; rep from * to last st, k1.
Row 2 (WS): K1, p2, *k2, p2; rep from * to last st, k1.
BO all sts loosely.

SLEEVES

Note: Sleeves are worked in the round. Use your favorite small circumference knitting needles and method. Continue stripe pattern as established.

Place 50 (57, 60, 68, 73, 81, 85) held sleeve sts back on needles to work in the rnd. CO 2 (2, 3, 3, 3, 3, 3) sts, pm for beg of rnd, CO 2 (2, 3, 3, 3, 3, 3) sts, knit to end of rnd—54 (61, 66, 74, 79, 87, 91) sts. Knit to m.

Work even in stripe patt for 14 rows. Sleeve measures approximately 2 in. / 5 cm.

Dec Rnd: K1, k2tog, knit to last 3 sts, ssk, k1—2 sts dec'd.

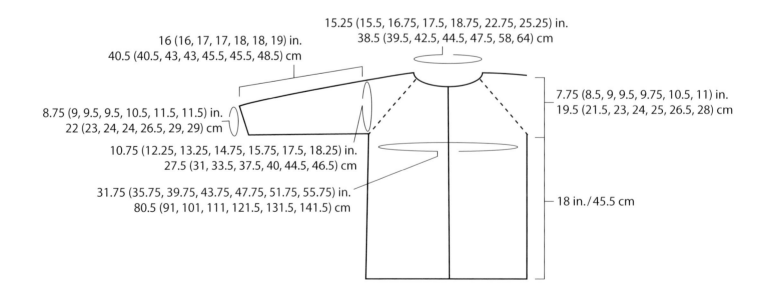

15.25 (15.5, 16.75, 17.5, 18.75, 22.75, 25.25) in.
38.5 (39.5, 42.5, 44.5, 47.5, 58, 64) cm

16 (16, 17, 17, 18, 18, 19) in.
40.5 (40.5, 43, 43, 45.5, 45.5, 48.5) cm

7.75 (8.5, 9, 9.5, 9.75, 10.5, 11) in.
19.5 (21.5, 23, 24, 25, 26.5, 28) cm

8.75 (9, 9.5, 9.5, 10.5, 11.5, 11.5) in.
22 (23, 24, 24, 26.5, 29, 29) cm

10.75 (12.25, 13.25, 14.75, 15.75, 17.5, 18.25) in.
27.5 (31, 33.5, 37.5, 40, 44.5, 46.5) cm

31.75 (35.75, 39.75, 43.75, 47.75, 51.75, 55.75) in.
80.5 (91, 101, 111, 121.5, 131.5, 141.5) cm

18 in. / 45.5 cm

Rep the Dec Rnd every 18 (10, 10, 6, 6, 6, 6)th rnd 4 (7, 8, 12, 12, 14, 16) more times—44 (45, 48, 48, 53, 57, 57) sts.

Continue in stripe patt until sleeve measures 13 (13, 14, 14, 15, 15, 16) in. / 33 (33, 35.5, 35.5, 38, 38, 40.5) cm ending with a CC stripe. Cut CC.

SLEEVE RIBBING

Work 3 in. / 7.5 cm of Ribbing with MC as follows:

Setup Rnd: K1, k2tog 0 (1, 0, 0, 1, 1, 1) times, p2, *k2, p2; rep from * to end—44 (44, 48, 48, 52, 56, 56) sts.

Next Rnd: *K2, p2; rep from * to end.

Cont in 2x2 ribbing as established until cuff measures 3 in. / 7.5 cm.

Rep for second sleeve.

FINISHING

RIGHT FRONT BUTTONBAND

With MC and RS of right front facing, pick up and knit 3 sts for every 4 rows up front edge— 132 (136, 140, 140, 144, 148, 148) sts. Work 3 in. / 7.5 cm of Ribbing as follows:

Ribbing Row 1 (WS): K1, p2, *k2, p2; rep from * to last st, k1.

Ribbing Row 2 (RS): Sl 1, k2, *p2, k2; rep from * to last st, k1.

LEFT FRONT BUTTONHOLE BAND

Mark placement of 12 buttonholes on left front, the lowest 1 in. / 2.5 cm from bottom edge, the highest 1 in. / 2.5 cm from top edge, and the remaining 10 evenly spaced in between.

With MC and RS of left front facing, pick up and knit 3 sts for every 4 rows down front edge—132 (136, 140, 140, 144, 148, 148) sts. Work 1.5 in. / 4 cm of Ribbing as follows:

Ribbing Row 1 (WS): Sl 1, p2, *k2, p2; rep from * to last st, k1.

Ribbing Row 2 (RS): K3, *p2, k2; rep from * to last st, k1.

Buttonhole Row (RS): Keeping in rib patt as established, BO2 opposite each marked buttonhole position.

Next Row (WS): Work in rib patt as established, CO2 over each buttonhole.

Cont in Ribbing as established until band measures 3 in. / 7.5 cm. BO all sts loosely.

COLLAR

With MC and WS of left front facing, pick up and knit 16 (17, 16, 16, 17, 17, 17) sts along left front band up front edge, then pick up 76 (78, 84, 88, 94, 114, 126) sts from neck CO, then pick up and knit 16 (17, 16, 16, 17, 17, 17) sts along right front band—108 (112, 116, 120, 128, 148, 160) sts. Work 3 in. / 7.5 cm of Ribbing as follows:

Next Row (WS): Sl 1, p2, *k2, p2; rep from * to last st, k1.

Next Row (RS): Sl 1, k2, *p2, k2; rep from * to last st, k1.

BO all sts loosely.

Seam up underarms. Sew buttons to right front buttonband opposite buttonholes. Weave in all ends. Block lightly to schematic measurements.

Maude

Pick three of your favorite bright and happy tones to blend with your favorite neutral to make this a sweater that will go with all your favorite clothes. Easy-to-work slip stitch patterning makes for a colorwork yoke that looks complicated but is dead simple to knit.

SIZE
Bust without bands: 30 (34, 38, 41.5, 45.5, 48.75, 52.75) in. / 76 (86.5, 96.5, 105.5, 115.5, 124, 134) cm
   Bust with bands buttoned: 31.75 (35.75, 39.75, 43.75, 47.75, 51.75, 55.75) in. / 80.5 (91, 101, 111, 121.5, 131.5, 141.5) cm

YARN
Knit Picks Wool of the Andes; Bulky weight; 100% wool; 137 yd. / 125 m, 3.5 oz. / 100 g per skein
   Marble Heather (MC): 4 (4, 4, 5, 6, 6, 7, 7) skeins
   Semolina (CC1): 1 (1, 1, 1, 1, 1, 2) skeins
   Amethyst Heather (CC2): 1 skein
   Marina (CC3): 1 skein

NEEDLES
US 10.5 (6.5 mm); adjust needle size as necessary to achieve gauge.

NOTIONS
- stitch markers
- tapestry needle
- waste yarn or stitch holder
- three 1-in. / 2.5-cm buttons

GAUGE
14 sts and 18.5 rows = 4 in. / 10 cm in St st

PATTERN STITCHES

Flat St st
  Row 1 (RS): Knit.
  Row 2 (WS): Purl.
  Rep Rows 1–2 for patt.
Flat Slip Stitch
  Row 1 (RS): K1, *sl 1, k1; rep from * to end.
  Row 2 (WS): P1, *sl 1, p1; rep from * to end.
Round St st
  Rnd 1: Knit.
  Rep Rnd 1 for patt.
Round Slip Stitch
  Rnd 1: *K1, sl 1; rep from * to end of rnd.
  Rep Rnd 1 for patt.

INSTRUCTIONS

YOKE

With MC, CO 57 (61, 65, 69, 73, 75, 79) sts.
Knit 2 rows.
With CC1, knit 2 rows. Break CC1.
With MC, knit 2 rows.

STRIPE ONE

With MC, work 2 rows of Flat St st.
Inc Row 1 (RS): With MC, k1, *M1, k2; rep from *
  to end—85 (91, 97, 103, 109, 112, 118) sts.
With MC, work 3 (5, 3, 5, 7, 5, 7) rows of
  Flat St st.

STRIPE TWO

With CC2, work 2 rows of Flat Slip Stitch.
With CC2, work 2 rows of Flat St st.
Inc Row 2 (RS): With CC2, k1, *M1, k3; rep from *
  to end—113 (121, 129, 137, 145, 149, 157) sts.
With CC2, work 3 rows of Flat St st. Break CC2.

STRIPE THREE

With MC, work 2 rows of Flat Slip Stitch.
With MC, work 2 rows of Flat St st.
Inc Row 3 (RS): With MC, k1, *M1, k4; rep from *
  to end—141 (151, 161, 171, 181, 186, 196) sts.
With MC, work 3 (3, 5, 5, 5, 7, 7) rows of
  Flat St st.

STRIPE FOUR

With CC3, work 2 rows of Flat Slip Stitch.
With CC3, work 2 rows of Flat St st.
Inc Row 4 (RS): With CC3, k1 (1, 1, 1, 1, 1, 8), *M1,
  k5 (5, 5, 5, 5, 5, 4); rep from * to end—169 (181,
  193, 205, 217, 223, 243) sts.
With CC3, work 3 rows of Flat St st. Break CC3.

STRIPE FIVE

With MC, work 2 rows of Flat Slip Stitch.
With MC, work 2 rows of Flat St st.

Sizes 30 (34, 45.5, 48.75, 52.75) Only

Inc Row 5 (RS): With MC, k9 (1, 1, 3, 13), *M1,
  k20 (10, 6, 5, 5); rep from * to end—177 (199,
  253, 267, 289) sts.

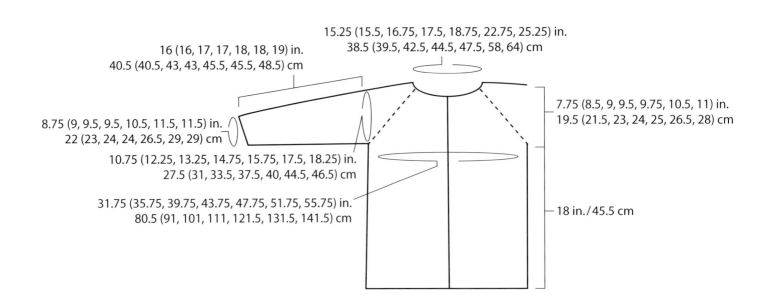

16 (16, 17, 17, 18, 18, 19) in.
40.5 (40.5, 43, 43, 45.5, 45.5, 48.5) cm

15.25 (15.5, 16.75, 17.5, 18.75, 22.75, 25.25) in.
38.5 (39.5, 42.5, 44.5, 47.5, 58, 64) cm

7.75 (8.5, 9, 9.5, 9.75, 10.5, 11) in.
19.5 (21.5, 23, 24, 25, 26.5, 28) cm

8.75 (9, 9.5, 9.5, 10.5, 11.5, 11.5) in.
22 (23, 24, 24, 26.5, 29, 29) cm

10.75 (12.25, 13.25, 14.75, 15.75, 17.5, 18.25) in.
27.5 (31, 33.5, 37.5, 40, 44.5, 46.5) cm

31.75 (35.75, 39.75, 43.75, 47.75, 51.75, 55.75) in.
80.5 (91, 101, 111, 121.5, 131.5, 141.5) cm

18 in./45.5 cm

Sizes 38 (41.5) Only
Inc Row 5 (RS): With MC, k2 (2), M1, k2 (3), *M1, k7 (k8); rep from * to end—221 (231) sts.

All Sizes
With MC, work 3 (3, 5, 5, 5, 7, 7) rows of Flat St st.

STRIPE SIX–DIVIDING STRIPE
With CC1, work 2 rows of Flat Slip Stitch.
Next Row (RS): With CC1, knit.
Dividing Row (WS): With CC1, p25 (28, 32, 34, 38, 40, 44), CO 2 (2, 2, 4, 4, 6, 6) sts, place 38 (42, 46, 46, 50, 52, 56) sts on waste yarn or st holder for sleeve, p51 (59, 65, 71, 77, 83, 89), CO 2 (2, 2, 4, 4, 6, 6) sts, place 38 (42, 46, 46, 50, 52, 56) sts on waste yarn or st holder for sleeve, p25 (28, 32, 34, 38, 40, 44)—105 (119, 133, 147, 161, 175, 189) sts for body; 38 (42, 46, 46, 50, 52, 56) sts on hold for each sleeve.

BODY
Beg with a RS row and with CC1, work 4 rows of Flat St st. Break CC1.

With MC, work 2 rows of Flat Slip Stitch.

Cont in MC only, work in Flat St st until body measures 14 (14, 14, 15, 15, 16, 16) in. / 35.5 (35.5, 35.5, 38, 38, 40.5, 40.5) cm, or approximately 3 in. / 7.5 cm less than desired body length. Work Hem Edging Rows as follows:

Rows 1–2: With MC, knit.
Rows 3–4: With CC1, knit.
Rows 5–6: With MC, knit.
Rows 7–8: With CC2, knit.
Rows 9–10: With MC, knit.
Rows 11–12: With CC3, knit.
Rows 13–14: With MC, knit.
BO all sts loosely.

SLEEVES

Note: Sleeves are worked in the round. Use your favorite small circumference knitting needles and method.

Place 38 (42, 46, 46, 50, 52, 56) held sleeve sts back on needles to work in the rnd. With CC1, CO 1 (1, 1, 2, 2, 3, 3) sts, pm, CO 1 (1, 1, 2, 2, 3, 3) sts—40 (44, 48, 50, 54, 58, 62) sts. Knit to m.

With CC1, work 4 rnds of Round St st. Break CC1.

With MC, work 2 rnds of Round Slip Stitch.

With MC, work 2 rnds of Round St st.

Dec Rnd: K1, k2tog, knit to last 3 sts, ssk, k1—2 sts dec'd.

Cont in Round St st, rep Dec Rnd every 8 (8, 6, 6, 6, 6, 4)th round 5 (6, 7, 7, 9, 10, 12) times more—28 (30, 32, 34, 34, 36, 36) sts.

Cont in Round St st until sleeve measures 13.5 (14, 14.5, 15, 15.5, 16, 16.5) in. / 34.5 (35.5, 37, 38, 39.5, 40.5, 42) cm, or approximately 3 in. / 7.5 cm less than desired sleeve length. Work Cuff Edging Rounds as follows:

Rnd 1: With MC, knit.
Rnd 2: With MC, purl.
Rnd 3: With CC1, knit.
Rnd 4: With CC1, purl.
Rnds 5–6: Rep Rnds 1–2.
Rnd 7: With CC2, knit.
Rnd 8: With CC2, purl.
Rnds 9–10: Rep Rnds 1–2.
Rnd 11: With CC3, knit.
Rnd 12: With CC3, purl.
Rnds 13–14: Rep Rnds 1–2.
BO all sts loosely.
Rep for second sleeve.

FINISHING

BUTTONBAND

With RS facing, MC, and beg at the collar and working toward the bottom edge, pick up and knit about 3 sts for every 4 rows.
Next Row (WS): Knit.
With CC1, knit 2 rows.
With MC, knit 2 rows.
BO all sts loosely.

BUTTONHOLE BAND

With RS facing, MC, and beg at the bottom edge and working toward the collar, pick up and knit about 3 sts for every 4 rows.
Next Row (WS): K25, pm, knit to end.
Buttonhole Row 1 (RS): With CC1, knit to m, (BO2, k7) twice, BO2, k2.
Buttonhole Row 2 (WS): With CC1, (knit to buttonhole, CO2) three times, knit to end. Break CC1.
With MC, knit 2 rows.
BO all sts loosely.

Sew up underarm seams. Sew buttons to left front buttonband opposite buttonholes. Weave in all ends. Block lightly to schematic measurements.

Zelma

Summery colors and simple slip stitch patterning make for a beautiful, wearable warm-weather tee. A-line shaping makes it flattering and easy to wear for all body types.

SIZE
Bust: 33.25 (37, 41.75, 45.5, 49.75, 53.5, 58.5) in. / 84.5 (94, 106, 115.5, 126.5, 136, 148.5) cm

YARN
Sweet Georgia Tough Love Sock; Fingering weight; 80% merino wool, 20% nylon; 425 yd. / 388 m, 4 oz. / 115 g per skein
  Lemon Curd (MC): 3 (3, 4, 4, 4, 4, 5) skeins
Party of Five Tough Love Sock; Fingering weight; 80% superwash merino wool, 20% nylon; 105 yd. / 96 m, 1 oz. / 28 g per skein
  Honey Fig Set (CCs): 1 (1, 1, 2, 2, 2, 2) sets

Note: If you are willing to use the contrast yarns a bit differently, you can easily use only one set for each size.

NEEDLES
US Size 7 (4.5 mm) for cast-on only.
US Size 4 (3.5 mm); adjust needle size to achieve gauge.

NOTIONS
- stitch markers
- waste yarn or stitch holders
- tapestry needle

GAUGE
26 sts and 36 rnds = 4 in. / 10 cm in St st

PATTERN STITCHES
St St in the Rnd
  Rnd 1: Knit.
  Rep Rnd 1 for patt.

NOTES

The contrast colors should be worked from darkest to lightest purple in the yoke, with the darkest being CC1 and so on. The yellow is the MC. You can carry the MC down if you like or cut it and join it new for each stripe. For the cuffs and hem, the colors will be worked in reverse order as indicated.

INSTRUCTIONS

YOKE

With CC1 and larger needle, CO 82 (90, 100, 110, 120, 134, 146) sts, pm and join to work in the rnd, being careful not to twist sts.

SECTION 1

Switch to smaller needles.

Rnd 1: Purl.
Rnd 2: With MC, *p1, sl 1 wyif; rep from * around.
Rnd 3: *Sl 1 wyif, p1; rep from * around.
Rnd 4: With CC1, knit.
Rnd 5: Purl.
Rnd 6: With MC, *yo, k1; rep from * to end of rnd—164 (180, 200, 220, 240, 268, 292) sts.
Rnds 7–9: Knit.
Rnd 10: With CC1, knit.
Rnd 11: Purl.

Rnd 12: With MC, *p1, sl 1 wyif; rep from * end of rnd.
Rnd 13: *Sl 1 wyif, p1; rep from * end of rnd.
Rnd 14: With CC1, knit.
Rnd 15: Purl. Cut CC1.
Rnd 16: With MC, *p1, sl 1 wyif; rep from * to end of rnd.
Rnd 17: *Sl 1 wyif, p1; rep from * to end of rnd.

SECTION 2

Rnd 1: With CC2, knit.
Rnd 2: Purl.
Rnd 3: With MC, *p1, sl 1 wyif; rep from * to end of rnd.
Rnd 4: *Sl 1 wyif, p1; rep from * to end of rnd.
Rnd 5: With CC2, knit.
Rnd 6: Purl. Cut CC2 or carry loosely up inside.
Rnd 7: With MC, *yo, k2; rep from * to end of rnd—246 (270, 300, 330, 360, 402, 438) sts.
Rnds 8–10: Knit.
Rnd 11: With CC2, knit.
Rnd 12: Purl.
Rnd 13: With MC, *p1, sl 1 wyif; rep from * to end of rnd.
Rnd 14: *Sl 1 wyif, p1; rep from * to end of rnd.
Rnd 15: With CC2, knit.
Rnd 16: Purl. Cut CC2.
Rnd 17: With MC, *p1, sl 1 wyif; rep from * to end of rnd.
Rnd 18: *Sl 1 wyif, p1; rep from * to end of rnd.

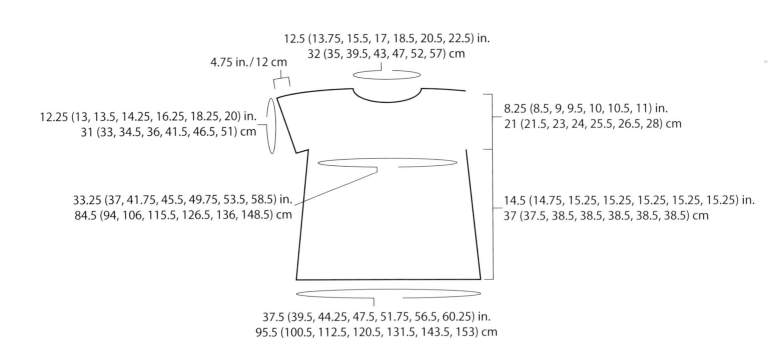

12.5 (13.75, 15.5, 17, 18.5, 20.5, 22.5) in.
32 (35, 39.5, 43, 47, 52, 57) cm

4.75 in./12 cm

12.25 (13, 13.5, 14.25, 16.25, 18.25, 20) in.
31 (33, 34.5, 36, 41.5, 46.5, 51) cm

8.25 (8.5, 9, 9.5, 10, 10.5, 11) in.
21 (21.5, 23, 24, 25.5, 26.5, 28) cm

33.25 (37, 41.75, 45.5, 49.75, 53.5, 58.5) in.
84.5 (94, 106, 115.5, 126.5, 136, 148.5) cm

14.5 (14.75, 15.25, 15.25, 15.25, 15.25, 15.25) in.
37 (37.5, 38.5, 38.5, 38.5, 38.5, 38.5) cm

37.5 (39.5, 44.25, 47.5, 51.75, 56.5, 60.25) in.
95.5 (100.5, 112.5, 120.5, 131.5, 143.5, 153) cm

SECTION 3

Work as for Section 2 using CC3 in place of CC2 and working Rnd 7 as follows:

Rnd 7: With MC, *yo, k3; rep from * to end of rnd—328 (360, 400, 440, 480, 536, 584) sts.

SECTION 4

Work as for Section 2 using CC4 in place of CC3, working Rnd 7 as follows and ending after Rnd 16.

Rnd 7: With MC, knit to end of rnd.

With MC, work St st in the Rnd until yoke measures 8.25 (8.5, 9, 9.5, 10, 10.5, 11) in. / 21 (21.5, 23, 24, 25.5, 26.5, 28) cm.

DIVIDE BODY AND SLEEVES

*K96 (108, 124, 138, 148, 162, 176) sts, place next 68 (72, 76, 82, 92, 106, 116) sts on waste yarn or st holder for sleeve, CO 6 (6, 6, 5, 7, 6, 7) sts, pm for side seam, CO 6 (6, 6, 5, 7, 6, 7) sts; rep from * once—216 (240, 272, 296, 324, 348, 380) sts for body; 68 (72, 76, 82, 92, 106, 116) sts on hold for each sleeve.

BODY

Work body in St st in the Rnd until body measures 4 in / 10 cm from underarm.

A-LINE SHAPING

Inc Rnd: *K1, M1, knit to 1 st before m, M1, k1; rep from * once—4 sts inc.

Rep Inc Rnd every 11 (24, 25, 38, 38, 19, 38)th rnd 6 (3, 3, 2, 2, 4, 2) more times—244 (256, 288, 308, 336, 368, 384) sts.

Work even until body measures 12.75 (13, 13.5, 13.5, 13.5, 13.5, 13.5) in. / 32.5 (33, 34.5, 34.5, 34.5, 34.5, 34.5) cm from underarm.

HEM

Rnd 1: With CC4, knit.
Rnd 2: Purl.
Rnd 3: With MC, *p1, sl 1 wyif; rep from * to end of rnd.
Rnd 4: *Sl 1 wyif, p1; rep from * to end of rnd.
Rnds 5–6: With CC3, rep Rnds 1–2.
Rnds 7–8: Rep Rnds 3–4.

Rnds 9-10: With CC2, rep Rnds 1-2.
Rnds 11-12: Rep Rnds 3-4.
Rnds 13-14: With CC1, rep Rnds 1-2.
BO all sts loosely.

SLEEVES

Note: Sleeves are worked in the round. Use your favorite small circumference knitting needles and method.

Place 68 (72, 76, 82, 92, 106, 116) held sleeve sts back on needle to work in the rnd. With MC, CO 6 (6, 6, 5, 7, 6, 7) sts, knit sleeve sts, CO 6 (6, 6, 5, 7, 6, 7) sts, pm for beg of rnd—80 (84, 88, 92, 106, 118, 130) sts.

Work St st in the Rnd for 3 in. / 7.5 cm.

HEM

Rnd 1: With CC4, knit.
Rnd 2: Purl.
Rnd 3: With MC, *p1, sl 1 wyif; rep from * to end of rnd.
Rnd 4: *Sl 1 wyif, p1; rep from * to end of rnd.
Rnds 5-6: With CC3, rep Rnds 1-2.
Rnds 7-8: Rep Rnds 3-4.
Rnds 9-10: With CC2, rep Rnds 1-2.
Rnds 11-12: Rep Rnds 3-4.
Rnds 13-14: With CC1, rep Rnds 1-2.
BO all sts loosely.
Rep for second sleeve.

FINISHING

Seam up underarms. Weave in all ends. Block lightly to schematic measurements.

Trudy

Gorgeous hand-dyed yarn makes the beautiful flame stitches come to life on this otherwise basic garter stitch tunic. Choose a fun multi-color for the contrast with a lovely tonal for the garter stitch body, for a lovely lightweight piece.

SIZE

Bust: 30.25 (34.25, 38.25, 42.25, 46.25, 50.25, 54.25) in. / 77 (87, 97, 107.5, 117.5, 127.5, 138) cm

YARN

Mrs. Crosby Satchel; Fingering weight; 100% merino wool; 370 yd. / 338 m, 3.5 oz. / 100 g per skein

Winter Wheat (MC): 3 (3, 3, 3, 4, 4, 5) skeins
Hot Pimiento (CC): 1 skein

NEEDLES

US Size 4 (3.5 mm); adjust needle size to achieve gauge.

NOTIONS

- stitch markers
- waste yarn or stitch holders
- tapestry needle

GAUGE

26 sts and 36 rnds = 4 in. / 10 cm in Garter st

PATTERN STITCHES

Garter st in the Rnd
  Rnd 1: Knit.
  Rnd 2: Purl.
  Rep Rnds 1–2 for patt.
Garter st Flat
  Row 1: Knit.
  Rep Row 1 for patt.

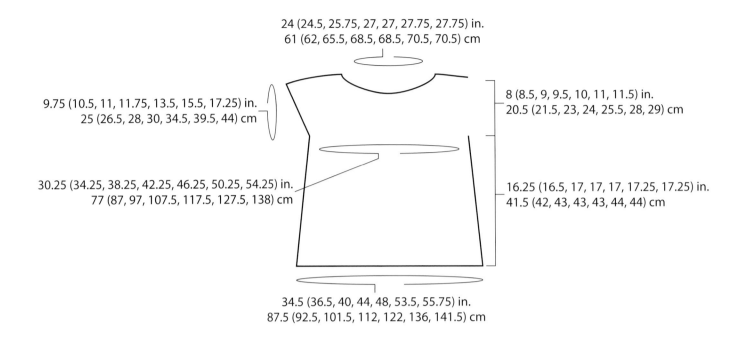

24 (24.5, 25.75, 27, 27, 27.75, 27.75) in.
61 (62, 65.5, 68.5, 68.5, 70.5, 70.5) cm

8 (8.5, 9, 9.5, 10, 11, 11.5) in.
20.5 (21.5, 23, 24, 25.5, 28, 29) cm

9.75 (10.5, 11, 11.75, 13.5, 15.5, 17.25) in.
25 (26.5, 28, 30, 34.5, 39.5, 44) cm

30.25 (34.25, 38.25, 42.25, 46.25, 50.25, 54.25) in.
77 (87, 97, 107.5, 117.5, 127.5, 138) cm

16.25 (16.5, 17, 17, 17, 17.25, 17.25) in.
41.5 (42, 43, 43, 43, 44, 44) cm

34.5 (36.5, 40, 44, 48, 53.5, 55.75) in.
87.5 (92.5, 101.5, 112, 122, 136, 141.5) cm

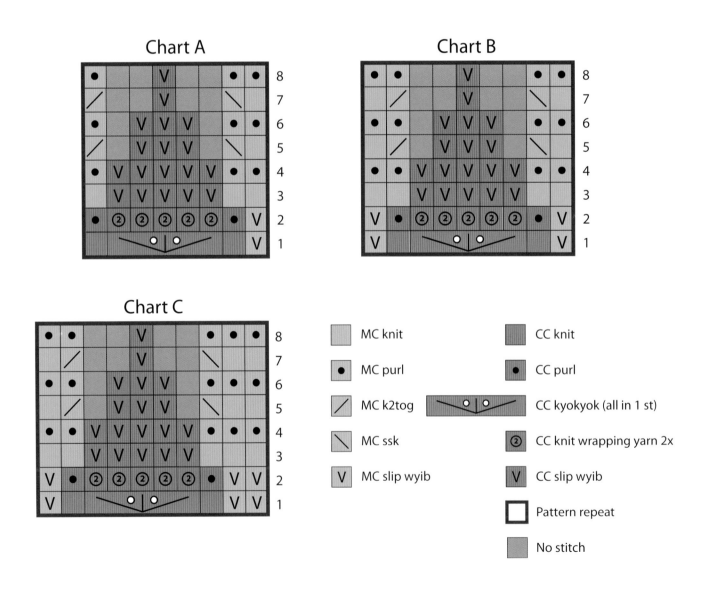

Chart A

Chart B

Chart C

MC knit		CC knit
• MC purl		• CC purl
╱ MC k2tog	CC kyokyok (all in 1 st)	
╲ MC ssk		② CC knit wrapping yarn 2x
V MC slip wyib		V CC slip wyib
		☐ Pattern repeat
		No stitch

INSTRUCTIONS

YOKE

With MC, CO 156 (160, 168, 176, 176, 180, 180) sts, pm, and join to work in the rnd, being careful not to twist sts.

Knit 1 rnd, purl 1 rnd.

FLAME PATT SECTION 1

Work Rnds 1–8 of Flame Chart A.

Size 30.25 Only
Inc Rnd 1: (Kfb, k1) twice, (kfb, k1, kfb, k2) 30 times, kfb, k1—219 sts.

Size 34.25 Only
Inc Rnd 1: Kfb, k2, *kfb, k1; rep from * to last 3 sts, kfb, k2—(239) sts.

Size 38.25 Only
Inc Rnd 1: *Kfb, k1; rep from * to end of rnd—(252) sts.

Sizes 42.25 (46.25) Only
Inc Rnd 1: (Kfb, k1) 29 (7) times, (kfb, k1, kfb) 20 (50) times, (kfb, k1) 29 (6) times—274 (289) sts.

Sizes 50.25 (54.25) Only
Inc Rnd 1: Kfb 27 (63) times, (kfb, k1, kfb) 42 (18) times, kfb 27 (63) times—318 (342) sts.

All Sizes
Purl 1 rnd. At end of rnd, sm, p4, pm to mark new beg of rnd. Keep original m in place for Division Rnd.

FLAME PATT SECTION 2

Setup Rnd: Work Rnd 1 of each chart the indicated number of times around. You may find it helpful to pm after each chart section. (*Note:* For size 38.25, you will work only Chart A.) Work Flame Chart B 1 (1, 0, 1, 1, 1, 1) time, Flame Chart A 26 (28, 63, 33, 71, 39, 42) times, Flame Chart B 1 (1, 0, 1, 0, 1, 1) time, Flame Chart A 25 (28, 0, 33, 0, 38, 41) times, and Flame Chart B 1 (1, 0, 0, 0, 0, 0) time each rnd.

Cont to work as set up through Rnd 8 of Charts A and B.

FLAME PATT SECTIONS 3, 4, 5

Size 30.25 Only
Inc Rnd 1: (Kfb, k2) twice, (kfb, k2, kfb, k3) 30 times, kfb, k2—282 sts.

Size 34.25 Only
Inc Rnd 1: Kfb, k3, *kfb, k2; rep from * to last 4 sts, kfb, k3—(318) sts.

Size 38.25 Only
Inc Rnd 1: *Kfb, k2; rep from * to end of rnd—(336) sts.

Sizes 42.25 (46.25) Only
Inc Rnd 1: (Kfb, k2) 29 (7) times, (kfb, k1, kfb, k2) 20 (50) times, (kfb, k2) 29 (6) times—(372, 402) sts.

Sizes 50.25 (54.25) Only
Inc Rnd 1: (Kfb, k1) 27 (63) times, (kfb, k1, kfb, k2) 42 (18) times, (kfb, k1) 27 (63) times—(456, 504) sts.

All Sizes
*Work Rnds 1–8 of Flame Chart C. At end of rnd, remove m, p4, pm to mark new beg of rnd.
   Knit 1 rnd, purl 1 rnd.
   Rep from * twice. Cut CC.
   Work Garter St in the Rnd for 14 (19, 23, 28, 32, 41, 46) more rows or until yoke measures approximately 8 (8.5, 9, 9.5, 10, 11, 11.5) in. / 20.5 (21.5, 23, 24, 25.5, 28, 29) cm. Cut MC and remove shifting beg of rnd m.

DIVIDE BODY AND ARMHOLES
Division Rnd: With MC and starting at original beg of rnd m, *k88 (101, 110, 123, 132, 145, 158) sts, CO 5 (5, 7, 7, 9, 9, 9) sts, pm for hip shaping, CO 5 (5, 7, 7, 9, 9, 9) sts, place next 53 (58, 58, 63, 69, 83, 94) sts on waste yarn or st holder for armhole; rep from * once, last m is new beg of rnd—196 (222, 248, 274, 300, 326, 352) body sts, 53 (58, 58, 63, 69, 83, 94) sts on hold for each armhole.

BODY
Work in Garter St in the Rnd until body measures 5 (8.25, 9.75, 9.75, 9.75, 7, 10) in. / 12.5 (21, 25, 25, 25, 18, 25.5) cm from underarm CO ending with a purl rnd.

HIP SHAPING
Note: Work next section for sizes 50.25 and 54.25. All other sizes move directly to All Sizes section.

Sizes 50.25 (54.25) Only
Inc Rnd: *Knit to 1 st before m, kfb, sm; rep from * once more—328 (354) sts.
Cont in Garter St in the Rnd for 7 rnds beg and ending with a purl rnd.

All Sizes
Inc Rnd: *K1, kfb, knit to 2 sts before next m, kfb, k1, sm; rep from * once more—4 sts inc'd.
Rep Inc Rnd approximately every 8th rnd on a knit row 6 (3, 2, 2, 2, 4, 1) more time(s)—224 (238, 260, 286, 312, 348, 362) sts.
Cont in Garter St in the Rnd until body measures 14 (14.25, 14.75, 14.75, 14.75, 15, 15) in. / 35.5 (36, 37.5, 37.5, 37.5, 38, 38) cm from underarm, ending with a purl rnd.

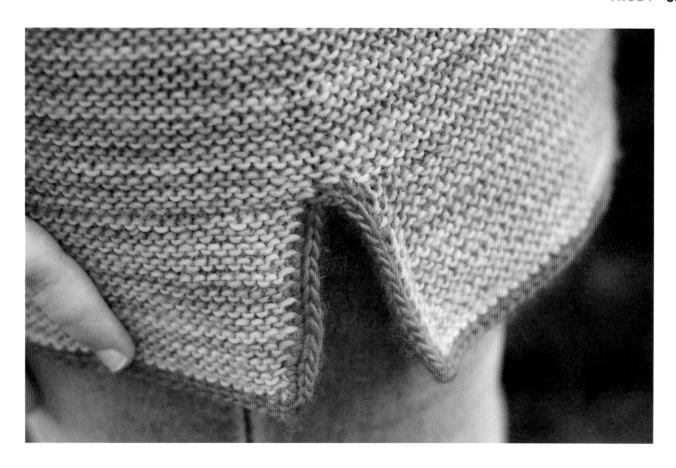

FINISHING

FRONT HEM

Next Row: Knit to m, turn. Place remaining sts on waste yarn for Back Hem—112 (119, 130, 143, 156, 174, 181) sts each flap.

Work Front Hem in Garter st Flat for 2 in. / 5 cm. Place sts on waste yarn for Bottom Trim. Cut MC.

BACK HEM

Place held Back Hem sts back on needles and work Garter St Flat for 2 in. / 5 cm. Cut MC.

BOTTOM TRIM

With CC, knit Back Hem sts, then pick up and knit 1 st for each garter ridge along left side of Back Hem, pick up and knit 1 st for each garter ridge down right side of Front Hem, place Front Hem sts back onto LH needle, knit Front Hem sts, pick up and knit 1 st for each garter ridge along left side of Front Hem, and then pick up and knit 1 st for each garter ridge along right side of Back Hem.

BO all sts loosely.

ARMHOLES

Note: Armholes are worked in the round. Use your favorite small circumference knitting needles and method.

Place 53 (58, 58, 63, 69, 83, 94) held armhole sts back on the needles to work in the rnd. With CC, RS facing, and beg in center of underarm, pick up and knit 5 (5, 7, 7, 9, 9, 9) sts, knit armhole sts; then pick up and knit 5 (5, 7, 7, 9, 9, 9) sts along underarm—63 (68, 72, 77, 87, 101, 112) sts.

BO all sts kwise. Rep for second armhole.

Weave in all ends. Block lightly to schematic measurements.

CHAPTER 4

Lovely and Lacy

There are many designs and motifs that you can make with knitting, but you can't beat the beauty of lace. It's time to put holes in your knitting—on purpose! Use yarn overs and artfully placed decreases to make up beautiful top-down sweaters with lace in the usual *and* unexpected places.

Idabelle

Yarn with a hint of sparkle in it is special enough, but add some pretty lace panels to the front of this sweater, and you have the perfect lightweight sweater to dress up or dress down.

SIZE
Bust: 36.75 (39.25, 42.25, 46.5, 50.25, 54.75, 56.75) in. / 93.5 (99.5, 107.5, 118, 127.5, 139, 144) cm

YARN
Crabapple Yarns Pizzazz; Fingering weight; 75% wool, 20% nylon, 5% other; 438 yd. / 400 m, 3.5 oz. / 100 g per skein
  Winesap: 4 (4, 5, 5, 5, 6, 6) skeins

NEEDLES
Body: US 4 (3.5 mm); ribbing: US 3 (3.25 mm); adjust needle size as necessary to achieve gauge.

NOTIONS
- stitch markers
- waste yarn or stitch holders
- eight ½-in. / 1.3-cm buttons
- tapestry needle

GAUGE
30 sts and 34 rows = 4 in. / 10 cm in St st

PATTERN STITCHES
Foliage Lace Pattern (also charted on page 60)
  Row 1 (RS): K5, p2tog, k2, yo, k5, yo, k2, p2tog, k2.
  Row 2 and all WS rows: Purl.
  Row 3: K4, p2tog, k2, yo, k1, yo, k2, p2tog, k7.
  Row 5: K3, p2tog, k2, yo, k3, yo, k2, p2tog, k6.
  Row 7: K2, p2tog, k2, yo, k5, yo, k2, p2tog, k5.
  Row 9: K7, p2tog, k2, yo, k1, yo, k2, p2tog, k4.
  Row 11: K6, p2tog, k2, yo, k3, yo, k2, p2tog, k3.
  Row 12: Purl.
  Rep Rows 1–12 for patt.

2x1 Rib Flat
   Row 1 (RS): K2, *p1, k2; rep from * to end.
   Row 2 (WS): P2, *k1, p2; rep from * to end.
   Rep Rows 1–2 for patt.
2x1 Rib in the Rnd
   Rnd 1: *K2, p1; rep from * to end of rnd.
   Rep Rnd 1 for patt.
St st in the Rnd
   Rnd 1: Knit.
   Rep Rnd 1 for patt.

NOTES

Cardigan is worked from the top down using raglan shaping to underarm. Sleeves are placed on hold and worked in the round later. Body is worked straight to ribbed hem. Stitches are picked up around neckline and ribbing is worked. Stitches are then picked up down both fronts to create buttonband and buttonhole band.

Foliage Lace pattern begins after neckline shaping is complete, and it is worked down both front edges.

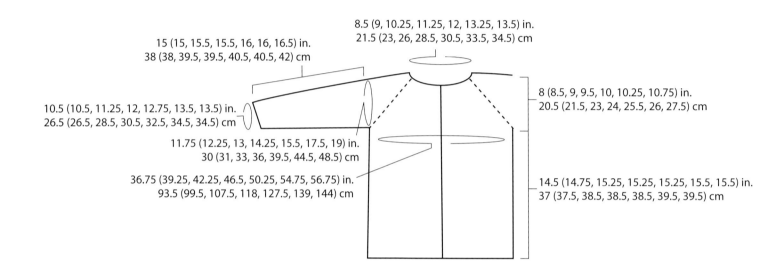

8.5 (9, 10.25, 11.25, 12, 13.25, 13.5) in.
21.5 (23, 26, 28.5, 30.5, 33.5, 34.5) cm

15 (15, 15.5, 15.5, 16, 16, 16.5) in.
38 (38, 39.5, 39.5, 40.5, 40.5, 42) cm

10.5 (10.5, 11.25, 12, 12.75, 13.5, 13.5) in.
26.5 (26.5, 28.5, 30.5, 32.5, 34.5, 34.5) cm

8 (8.5, 9, 9.5, 10, 10.25, 10.75) in.
20.5 (21.5, 23, 24, 25.5, 26, 27.5) cm

11.75 (12.25, 13, 14.25, 15.5, 17.5, 19) in.
30 (31, 33, 36, 39.5, 44.5, 48.5) cm

36.75 (39.25, 42.25, 46.5, 50.25, 54.75, 56.75) in.
93.5 (99.5, 107.5, 118, 127.5, 139, 144) cm

14.5 (14.75, 15.25, 15.25, 15.25, 15.5, 15.5) in.
37 (37.5, 38.5, 38.5, 38.5, 39.5, 39.5) cm

Foliage Lace Pattern

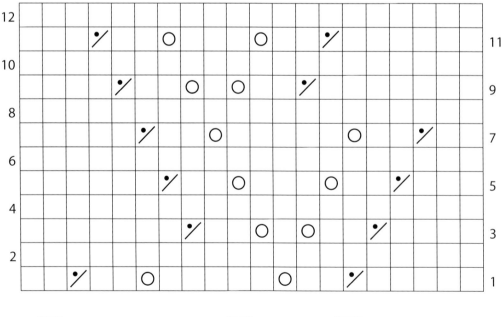

Knit on RS, purl on WS   O   Yarn over   ⟋ Purl 2 together

INSTRUCTIONS

YOKE

CO 63 (67, 77, 84, 90, 99, 101) sts.

Setup Row (WS): P2 for front, pm, p1, pm, p10 (10, 14, 16, 16, 18, 18) for sleeve, pm, p1, pm, p35 (39, 41, 44, 50, 55, 57) for back, pm, p1, pm, p10 (10, 14, 16, 16, 18, 18) for sleeve, pm, p1, pm, p2 for front.

SHAPING A

Note: Front, back, neckline, and sleeve shaping happen **AT THE SAME TIME**. Read through the next sections carefully. You will inc each front, sleeve, and back section. You will also be shaping the neckline and beg to work the 20-st Foliage Lace patt.

Inc Row 1 (RS): *Knit to m, yo, sm, k1, sm, yo; rep from * 3 times—8 sts inc; 1 st inc each front, 2 sts inc each sleeve and back.

Next Row: Purl.

Rep last 2 rows 24 (25, 25, 24, 25, 22, 24) times.

Inc Row 2 (RS): *Knit to 2 sts before marker, M1, k2, yo, sm, k1, sm, yo, knit to marker, yo, sm, k1, sm, yo, k2, M1; rep from * once—12 sts inc; 2 sts inc each front and sleeve, 4 sts inc back.

Next Row: Purl.

Rep last 2 rows 6 (7, 10, 13, 13, 13, 11) times.

Inc Row 3 (RS): *Knit to 2 sts before m, M1, k2, yo, sm, k1, sm, yo, k2, M1, knit to 2 sts before m, M1, k2, yo, sm, k1, sm, yo, k2, M1; rep from * once—16 sts inc; 2 sts inc each front, 4 sts inc each sleeve and back.

Next Row: Purl.

Rep last 2 rows 1 (1, 0, 0, 1, 5, 7) time(s).

AT THE SAME TIME . . .

SHAPING B

Work Shaping A until front section measures 3.5 in. / 9 cm from cast-on, ending on a WS row.

  Note: You are now going to inc sts along the neckline while continuing to work Shaping A above.

Sizes 50.25 (54.75, 56.75) Only

Inc Row (RS): K1, M1, work Shaping A as established to last st, M1, k1—1 st inc each neck edge.

Next Row: Purl.

Work last 2 rows 9 (8, 8) times total—9 (8, 8) sts inc each neck edge.

All Sizes

Inc Row (RS): CO 1 (1, 1, 1, 2, 2, 2) st(s), work Shaping A as established to end, CO 1 (1, 1, 1, 2, 2, 2) st(s)—1 (1, 1, 1, 2, 2, 2) st(s) inc each neck edge.

Next Row: Purl.

Rep last 2 rows 4 (6, 8, 10, 1, 2, 2) time(s) total—4 (6, 8, 10, 2, 4, 4) sts inc each neck edge.

Next 2 Rows: CO 20 sts, work Shaping A as established to end—24 (26, 28, 30, 31, 32, 32) sts total inc each neck edge.

Lace Patt Setup Row (RS): Work 20-st Foliage Lace patt, work Shaping A as established to last 20 sts, work 20-st Foliage Lace patt.

When all shaping is complete—427 (455, 489, 528, 560, 611, 637) sts; 69 (74, 80, 87, 91, 97, 99) sts each front, 82 (86, 92, 98, 104, 116, 124) sts each sleeve, 121 (131, 141, 154, 166, 181, 187) sts back, and 4 seam sts.

DIVIDE BODY AND SLEEVES

Division Row (RS): Work 20-st Foliage Lace patt, knit to m, remove m, k1, remove m, place next 82 (86, 92, 98, 104, 116, 124) sts on waste yarn or st holder for sleeve, remove m, CO 6 (6, 6, 8, 12, 16, 18) sts, k1, remove m, knit across back sts to next m, remove m, k1, place next 82 (86, 92, 98, 104, 116, 124) sts on waste yarn or st holder for sleeve, remove m, CO 6 (6, 6, 8, 12, 16, 18) sts, k1, remove m, knit to last 20 sts, work 20-st Foliage Lace patt—275 (295, 317, 348, 376, 411, 425) sts.

BODY

Work even in established patts until body measures 12.5 (12.75, 13.25, 13.25, 13.25, 13.5, 13.5) in. / 32 (32.5, 33.5, 33.5, 33.5, 34.5, 34.5) cm from underarm CO.

HEM

Work 2x1 Rib Flat for 2 in. / 5 cm.
BO all sts loosely in patt.

SLEEVES

Note: Sleeves are worked in the round. Use your favorite small circumference knitting needles and method.

Place 82 (86, 92, 98, 104, 116, 124) held sleeve sts back on the needle to work in the rnd, CO 3 (3, 3, 4, 6, 8, 9) sts, knit sleeve sts, CO 3 (3, 3, 4, 6, 8, 9) sts, pm for beg of rnd—88 (92, 98, 106, 116, 132, 142) sts.

Work St st in the Rnd for 34 (34, 34, 26, 17, 17, 17) rnds or until sleeve measures approximately 4 (4, 4, 3, 2, 2, 2) in. / 10 (10, 10, 7.5, 5, 5, 5) cm.

Dec Rnd: K1, ssk, knit to last 3 sts, k2tog, k1—2 sts dec'd.

Rep Dec Rnd every 17 (12, 12, 12, 10, 7, 5) rnds 4 (6, 6, 7, 9, 14, 19) times more—78 (78, 84, 90, 96, 102, 102) sts.

Work even until sleeve measures 13 (13, 13.5, 13.5, 14, 14, 14.5) in. / 33 (33, 34.5, 34.5, 35.5, 35.5, 37) cm from underarm.

CUFF

Work 2x1 Rib in the Rnd for 2 in. / 5 cm.
BO all sts loosely in patt.
Rep for second sleeve.

FINISHING

RIBBED COLLAR

With RS facing, smaller needles, and beg at edge of right front neckline, pick up and knit 20 sts from neck CO, pick up and knit 45 (47, 51, 54, 54, 55, 56) sts along edge of front neckline and sleeve, pick up and knit 34 (39, 40, 43, 49, 56, 57) sts along back neck edge, pick up and knit 45 (47, 51, 54, 54, 55, 56) sts along left sleeve and front neckline, and then pick up and knit 20 sts from neck CO—164 (173, 182, 191, 197, 206, 209) sts.

Work 2x1 Rib Flat for 1.5 in. / 4 cm.
BO all sts loosely in patt.

LEFT FRONT BUTTONBAND

With RS facing and using smaller needles, pick up and knit approximately 149 (152, 161, 164, 167, 173, 176) sts along Left Front.

Work 2x1 Rib Flat for 1.5 in. / 4 cm.
BO all sts loosely in patt.

RIGHT FRONT BUTTONHOLE BAND

Mark placement of 8 buttonholes on left front, the lowest 1 in. / 2.5 cm from bottom edge, the highest 1 in. / 2.5 cm from top edge, and the remaining 6 evenly spaced in between.

 With RS facing and smaller needles, pick up and knit approximately 149 (152, 161, 164, 167, 173, 176) sts along Right Front.

 Work 2x1 Rib Flat for 0.5 in. / 1.5 cm.

Buttonhole Row (RS): Keeping in rib patt as established, BO2 opposite each marked buttonhole position.

Next Row (WS): Work in rib patt as established, CO2 over each buttonhole.

Continue in 2x1 Rib Flat until band measures 1.5 in. / 4 cm from pick-up row.

BO all sts loosely in patt.

 Sew up underarms. Weave in all ends. Block lightly to schematic measurements. Sew buttons opposite buttonholes.

Flora

Wrap yourself up in the beautiful shawl collar of this open-front cardigan and secure it with your favorite shawl pin. Cozy worsted weight yarn makes it a fast, fun knit.

SIZE
Bust: 32.75 (36.75, 40.75, 44.75, 48.75, 52.75, 56.75) in. / 83 (93.5, 103.5, 113.5, 124, 134, 144) cm

YARN
Knit Picks Preciosa; Worsted weight; 100% merino wool; 273 yd. / 250 m, 3.5 oz. / 100 g per skein

Anemone: 5 (5, 6, 6, 7, 7, 8) skeins

NEEDLES
US 7 (4.5 mm); adjust needle size as necessary to achieve gauge.

NOTIONS
- stitch markers
- waste yarn or stitch holders
- tapestry needle

GAUGE
20 sts and 29 rows = 4 in. / 10 cm in St st

PATTERN STITCHES
Lace (also charted on page 66)

Row 1 (RS): Sl 1, kyok, k3, *p3, k3; rep from * to last st, k1—2 sts inc'd.

Row 2: Sl 1, *p3, k3; rep from * to last st, k1.

Row 3: Sl 1, kyok, k2, yo, s2kp, yo, *k3, yo, s2kp, yo; rep from * to last st, k1—2 sts inc'd.

Row 4: Sl 1, *k3, p3; rep from * to last 3 sts, k3.

Row 5: Sl 1, kyok, p1, *k3, p3; rep from * to last st, k1—2 sts inc'd.

Row 6: Sl 1, *k3, p3; rep from * to last 5 sts, k3, p1, k1.

Row 7: Sl 1, kyok, k3, *yo, s2kp, yo, k3; rep from * to last sts, k1—2 sts inc'd.

Row 8: Sl 1, *p3, k3; rep from * to last st, k1.

Row 9: Sl 1, kyok, p2, k3, *p3, k3; rep from * to last st, k1—2 sts inc'd.

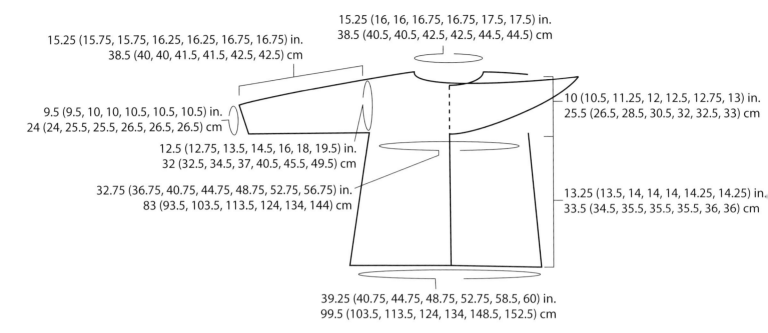

15.25 (16, 16, 16.75, 16.75, 17.5, 17.5) in.
38.5 (40.5, 40.5, 42.5, 42.5, 44.5, 44.5) cm

15.25 (15.75, 15.75, 16.25, 16.25, 16.75, 16.75) in.
38.5 (40, 40, 41.5, 41.5, 42.5, 42.5) cm

10 (10.5, 11.25, 12, 12.5, 12.75, 13) in.
25.5 (26.5, 28.5, 30.5, 32, 32.5, 33) cm

9.5 (9.5, 10, 10, 10.5, 10.5, 10.5) in.
24 (24, 25.5, 25.5, 26.5, 26.5, 26.5) cm

12.5 (12.75, 13.5, 14.5, 16, 18, 19.5) in.
32 (32.5, 34.5, 37, 40.5, 45.5, 49.5) cm

13.25 (13.5, 14, 14, 14, 14.25, 14.25) in.
33.5 (34.5, 35.5, 35.5, 35.5, 36, 36) cm

32.75 (36.75, 40.75, 44.75, 48.75, 52.75, 56.75) in.
83 (93.5, 103.5, 113.5, 124, 134, 144) cm

39.25 (40.75, 44.75, 48.75, 52.75, 58.5, 60) in.
99.5 (103.5, 113.5, 124, 134, 148.5, 152.5) cm

Lace Pattern

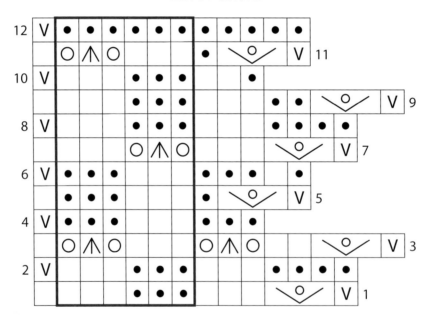

	Knit on RS, purl on WS		kyok–knit, yarn over, knit in same st
●	Purl on RS, knit on WS		s2kp–slip 2 sts together knitwise, k1, pass both slipped sts over
V	Slip 1		Pattern repeat
O	Yarn over		

Row 10: Sl 1, *p3, k3; rep from * to last 3 sts, p2, k1.
Row 11: Sl 1, kyok, p1, *k3, yo, s2kp, yo; rep from * to last st, k1—2 sts inc'd.
Row 12: Sl 1, knit to end.
Rep Rows 1–12 for patt.

Body Pattern
Row 1 (RS): Sl 1, knit to end.
Row 2 (WS): Sl 1, k3, purl to last 4 sts, k4.
Rows 3–10: Rep Rows 1–2.
Rows 11–14: Rep Row 1.
Rep Rows 1–14 for patt.

Sleeve Pattern
Rnds 1–11: Knit.
Rnd 12: Purl.
Rnd 13: Knit.
Rnd 14: Purl.
Rep Rnds 1–14 for patt.

Garter st Flat
Row 1: Knit.
Rep Row 1 for patt.

Garter st in the Rnd
Rnd 1: Knit.
Rnd 2: Purl.
Rep Rnds 1–2 for patt.

St st Flat
Row 1 (RS): Knit.
Row 2 (WS): Purl.
Rep Rows 1–2 for patt.

NOTES

A shawl-like yoke is created using increases at the beginning of every other row. Shawl extension will wrap and rest over one shoulder. After yoke, stitches are divided to work the body, while sleeve stitches are placed on hold and worked after completion of body. Slip all stitches purlwise with yarn in the back on right side rows and yarn in the front on wrong side rows.

INSTRUCTIONS

YOKE

CO 76 (80, 80, 84, 84, 88, 88) sts. Knit 1 row.
Inc Row 1 (RS): Sl 1, kyok, k2, *yo, k2; rep from * to end—114 (120, 120, 126, 126, 132, 132) sts.
Next Row: Sl 1, knit to end.

Work Lace Rows 1–12 once—126 (132, 132, 138, 138, 144, 144) sts.

Inc Row 2 (RS): Sl 1, kyok, k3 (2, 2, 3, 2, 2, 2), *yo, k2; rep from * to last 5 (0, 0, 5, 6, 0, 0) sts, knit to end—186 (198, 198, 204, 204, 216, 216) sts.

Next Row: Sl 1, knit to end.

Work Lace Rows 1–12 once—198 (210, 210, 216, 216, 228, 228) sts.

Inc Row 3 (RS): Sl 1, kyok, k5 (0, 0, 4, 1, 1, 1), *yo, k3 (3, 3, 2, 2, 2, 2); rep from * to last 5 (1, 1, 4, 1, 1, 1) sts, yo, knit to end—258 (282, 282, 318, 324, 342, 342) sts.

Next Row: Sl 1, knit to end.

Work Lace Rows 1–12 once—270 (294, 294, 330, 336, 354, 354) sts.

Inc Row 4 (RS): Sl 1, kyok, k6 (6, 2, 2, 2, 2, 2), *yo, k4 (4, 3, 3, 3, 3, 2); rep from * to last 6 (6, 2, 2, 8, 8, 8) sts, knit to end—330 (360, 390, 438, 444, 468, 522) sts.

Next Row: Sl 1, knit to end.

Work Lace Rows 1–12 once—342 (372, 402, 450, 456, 480, 534) sts.

Work even in St st Flat for 16 (20, 26, 32, 34, 36, 38) more rows, ending on a WS row. Yoke measures approximately 10 (10.5, 11.25, 12, 12.5, 12.75, 13) in. / 25.5 (26.5, 28.5, 30.5, 32, 32.5, 33) cm.

DIVIDE BODY AND SLEEVES

Division Row (RS): BO 70 (76, 94, 114, 92, 76, 94) sts (1 st rem on needle), k38 (43, 46, 51, 55, 60, 65), *place next 58 (60, 60, 64, 70, 80, 88) sts on waste yarn or st holder for sleeve, CO 2 (2, 4, 4, 5, 5, 5) sts, pm, CO 2 (2, 4, 4, 5, 5, 5) sts**, k78 (88, 94, 104, 112, 122, 132); rep from * to ** once, knit to end—164 (184, 204, 224, 244, 264, 284) sts.

BODY

Next Row (WS): Sl 1, k3, purl to last 4 sts, k4.

Work Body Pattern starting on Row 3 for 2 in. / 5 cm from underarm, ending on a WS row.

Inc Row (RS): Sl 1, *work Body Pattern to 1 st before m, M1, k1, sm, k1, M1; rep from * once, work in Body Pattern to end—4 sts inc'd.

Cont in Body Pattern, rep Inc Row every 8 (14, 16, 16, 16, 12, 20)th row 7 (4, 4, 4, 4, 6, 3) more times—196 (204, 224, 244, 264, 292, 300) sts.

Cont in Body Pattern until Body measures approximately 12.25 (12.5, 13, 13, 13, 13.25, 13.25) in. / 31 (32, 33, 33, 33, 33.5, 33.5) cm, or 1 in. / 2.5 cm from desired length from underarm.

Work Garter st Flat for 6 rows.

BO all sts loosely.

SLEEVES

Note: Sleeves are worked in the round. Use your favorite small circumference knitting needles and method.

Place 58 (60, 60, 64, 70, 80, 88) held sleeve sts back on the needles to work in the rnd. CO 2 (2, 4, 4, 5, 5, 5) sts, knit across sleeve sts, cast on 2 (2, 4, 4, 5, 5, 5) sts, pm for beg of rnd.

Work Sleeve Pattern starting on Rnd 3 until Sleeve measures 2 in. / 5 cm.

Dec Rnd: K1, k2tog, knit to last 3 sts, ssk, k1—2 sts dec'd.

Cont in Sleeve Pattern, rep Dec Rnd every 11 (10, 9, 8, 6, 4, 4)th rnd 6 (7, 8, 10, 13, 18, 22) more times—48 (48, 50, 50, 52, 52, 52) sts.

Cont in Sleeve Pattern until Sleeve measures approximately 14.25 (14.75, 14.75, 15.25, 15.25, 15.75, 15.75) in. / 36 (37.5, 37.5, 38.5, 38.5, 40, 40) cm, or 1 in. / 2.5 cm short of desired length from underarm.

CUFF

Work Garter St in the Rnd for 6 rnds.

BO all sts loosely.

Rep for second sleeve.

FINISHING

Sew up underarm seams. Weave in all ends. Block lightly to schematic measurements.

Odette

Knit up a short-sleeve wardrobe staple with simple lace and a statement button. You need only one, so choose something special.

SIZE
Bust: 31.75 (35.75, 39.75, 44.25, 48.25, 51.75, 56.25) in. / 80.5 (91, 101, 112.5, 122.5, 131.5, 143) cm

YARN
Patons Classic Wool DK; DK weight; 100% wool; 125 yd. / 114 m, 1.8 oz. / 50 g per skein
  Wisteria: 8 (10, 11, 12, 14, 15, 16) skeins

NEEDLES
US 6 (4.0 mm); adjust needle size as necessary to achieve gauge.

NOTIONS
- stitch markers
- tapestry needle
- waste yarn or stitch holders
- one ¾-in. / 1.9-cm button

GAUGE
22 sts and 32 Rows = 4 in. / 10 cm in St st

PATTERN STITCHES
Stockinette Stitch
  Rnd 1: Knit.
  Rep Rnd 1 for patt.

SPECIAL ABBREVIATION
c3 (cluster 3): Sl 1, k2, pass sl st over
  both—1 st dec'd.

INSTRUCTIONS

YOKE

CO 119 (125, 131, 131, 137, 137, 143) sts, do not join.

Row 1 (WS): Sl 1, knit to end.

Repeat last row twice more.

Buttonhole Row (RS): Sl 1, k1, yo, k2tog, knit to end.

Rep Row 1 four more times.

Work 4 (4, 4, 4, 5, 5, 5) reps of the following 14-Row Yoke Lace Pattern, then work Rows 1–8 (10, 12, 12, 4, 8, 12) once more. Incorporate the Inc Row as directed on the first row.

YOKE LACE PATTERN

Row 1 (RS): Work Inc Row as directed below for each repeat.

Row 2 (WS): Sl 1, k3, purl to last 4 sts, k4.

Row 3: Sl 1, k4, *yo, ssk, rep from * to last 6 sts, k6.

Row 4: Sl 1, knit to end.

Row 5: Rep Row 3.

Row 6: Rep Row 2.

Row 7: Sl 1, knit to end.

Row 8: Rep Row 2.

Row 9: Sl 1, k4, *c3, yo, rep from * to last 6 sts, k6.

Row 10: Rep Row 2.

Row 11: Sl 1, k5, *yo, c3; rep from * to last 5 sts, k5.

Row 12: Rep Row 2.

Row 13: Rep Row 9.

Row 14: Sl 1, k3, purl to last 4 sts, k4.

Inc Row (First Rep): Sl 1, k6 (9, 3, 3, 6, 6, 9), M1, *k3, M1; rep from * to last 7 (10, 4, 4, 7, 7, 10) sts, knit to end—155 (161, 173, 173, 179, 179, 185) sts.

Inc Row (Second Rep): Sl 1, k4 (10, 4, 6, 9, 9, 3), M1, *k5 (4, 4, 3, 3, 3, 3), M1; rep from * to last 5 (10, 4, 7, 10, 10, 4) sts, knit to end—185 (197, 215, 227, 233, 233, 245) sts.

Inc Row (Third Rep): Sl 1, k5 (10, 4, 19, 13, 22, 16), M1, *k6 (5, 5, 4, 5, 4, 4), M1; rep from * to last 5 (11, 5, 19, 14, 22, 16) sts, knit to end—215 (233, 257, 275, 275, 281, 299) sts.

Inc Row (Fourth Rep): Sl 1, k5 (11, 5, 19, 14, 22, 16), M1, *k7 (6, 6, 5, 6, 5, 5), M1; rep from * to last 6 (11, 5, 20, 14, 23, 17) sts, knit to end—245 (269, 299, 323, 317, 329, 353) sts.

Inc Row (Fifth Rep): Sl 1, k6 (11, 8, 20, 14, 5, 28), M1, *k8 (6, 6, 6, 7, 6, 5), M1; rep from * to last 6 (11, 8, 20, 15, 5, 29) sts, knit to end—275 (311, 347, 371, 359, 383, 413) sts.

Sizes 48.25 (51.75, 56.25) Only

Inc Row (Sixth Rep): Sl 1, k15 (5, 29), M1, *k8 (7, 6), M1; rep from * to last 15 (6, 29) sts, knit to end—401 (437, 473) sts.

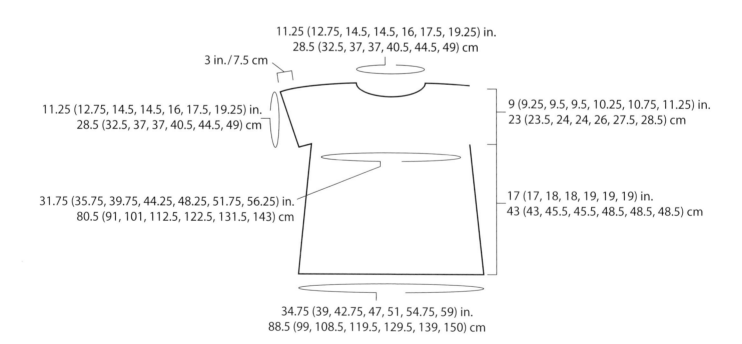

11.25 (12.75, 14.5, 14.5, 16, 17.5, 19.25) in.
28.5 (32.5, 37, 37, 40.5, 44.5, 49) cm

3 in./7.5 cm

11.25 (12.75, 14.5, 14.5, 16, 17.5, 19.25) in.
28.5 (32.5, 37, 37, 40.5, 44.5, 49) cm

9 (9.25, 9.5, 9.5, 10.25, 10.75, 11.25) in.
23 (23.5, 24, 24, 26, 27.5, 28.5) cm

31.75 (35.75, 39.75, 44.25, 48.25, 51.75, 56.25) in.
80.5 (91, 101, 112.5, 122.5, 131.5, 143) cm

17 (17, 18, 18, 19, 19, 19) in.
43 (43, 45.5, 45.5, 48.5, 48.5, 48.5) cm

34.75 (39, 42.75, 47, 51, 54.75, 59) in.
88.5 (99, 108.5, 119.5, 129.5, 139, 150) cm

DIVIDE BODY AND SLEEVES

Next Rnd: K40 (46, 50, 56, 61, 66, 71), place 56 (63, 72, 72, 78, 86, 94) sts on waste yarn or st holder for sleeve, CO 3 (3, 4, 4, 5, 5, 6) sts, pm for beg of rnd, CO 3 (4, 4, 4, 5, 5, 6) sts, k83 (93, 103, 115, 123, 133, 143), place 56 (63, 72, 72, 78, 86, 94) sts on waste yarn or st holder for sleeve, CO 3 (4, 4, 4, 5, 5, 6) sts, pm for waist shaping, CO 3 (3, 4, 4, 5, 5, 6) sts, knit to end of rnd—175 (199, 219, 243, 265, 285, 309) sts for body. Join for knitting in the rnd.

BODY

Knit even for 24 rnds. Body measures approximately 3 in. / 7.5 cm from underarm.
Inc Rnd: K1, M1, knit to 1 st before waist m, M1, k1, sm, k1, M1, knit to 1 st before end of rnd, M1, k1—4 sts inc'd.
Rep Inc Rnd every 24th rnd, or every 3 in. / 7.5 cm, three more times—191 (215, 235, 259, 281, 301, 325) sts. Work in St st until body measures 16 (16, 17, 17, 18, 18, 18) in. / 40.5 (40.5, 43, 43, 45.5, 45.5, 45.5) cm from underarm or 1 in. / 2.5 cm less than desired length.
Work garter stitch hem as follows:
Rnd 1: Knit.
Rnd 2: Purl.
Rep last 2 rnds five times. BO all sts loosely.

SLEEVES

Note: Sleeves are worked in the round. Use your favorite small circumference knitting needles and method.
Place 56 (63, 72, 72, 78, 86, 94) held sleeve sts back on needles to work in the rnd. CO 3 (4, 4, 4, 5, 5, 6) sts, pm for beg of rnd, CO 3 (3, 4, 4, 5, 5, 6) sts, knit to beg of rnd—62 (70, 80, 80, 88, 96, 106) sts. Work in St st until sleeve measures 2 in. / 5 cm from underarm. Work garter stitch hem as follows:
Rnd 1: Knit.
Rnd 2: Purl.
Rep last 2 rnds five times. BO all sts loosely.

FINISHING

Seam up underarms. Weave in all ends. Block lightly to schematic measurements. Sew button at back neck opposite buttonhole.

Constance

This reversible sweater is a cozy cold-weather piece that knits up in a flash in bulky yarn. Wearing the lace on the back is an unexpected look, but you can easily wear it either way to suit your mood!

SIZE
Bust: 30.5 (35.75, 40.75, 45.75, 51, 56, 61) in. / 77.5 (91, 103.5, 116, 129.5, 142, 155) cm

YARN
Patons Classic Wool Bulky; Bulky weight; 100% wool; 78 yd. / 71 m; 3.5 oz. / 100 g per skein
   Geyser Blue: 7 (9, 10, 11, 13, 14, 15) skeins

NEEDLES
Size 11 (8.0 mm); adjust needle size as necessary to achieve gauge.

NOTIONS
- stitch markers
- tapestry needle
- waste yarn or stitch holders

GAUGE
11 sts and 16 rnds to 4 in. / 10 cm in St st

PATTERN STITCHES
Wide Garter Rib
   Rnd 1: Knit.
   Rnd 2: *K2, p2, k3; rep from *.
Lace Pattern (also charted on page 78)
   Rnd 1: *K1, yo, k1, s2kp, k1, yo, k1; rep from *.
   Rnd 2: *P1, k5, p1; rep from *.
   Rnd 3: *K2, yo, s2kp, yo, k2; rep from *.
   Rnd 4: *P1, k5, p1; rep from *.
   Rnd 5: Knit.
   Rnd 6: *P1, k5, p1; rep from *.
St st in the Rnd
   Rnd 1: Knit.
   Rep Rnd 1 for patt.

NOTES
The sleeves are worked in stockinette stitch. The front is worked in a wide garter rib and the back is worked in a lace pattern that mimics the wide garter rib. Slip markers when you come to them.

INSTRUCTIONS

YOKE

CO 54 (57, 60, 63, 75, 84, 93) sts, pm and join to work in the rnd, being careful not to twist sts.

Ribbing Rnd: *K2, p1; rep from * to end of rnd. Rep last rnd 7 (7, 7, 5, 5, 5, 3) more times.

Note: Work the following Transition Rnd as follows: If increase (inc) falls on a knit st, work an M1. If inc falls on a purl st, work pfb.

Transition Rnd: Work in established patt for 2 (2, 0, 4, 2, 2, 2) sts, *inc, work in established patt for 5 (6, 6, 6, 8, 8, 8) sts; rep from * to end of rnd—64 (66, 70, 72, 84, 94, 104) sts.

Setup Rnd 1: *K11 (9, 7, 5, 7, 9, 10) (sleeve), pm, k3 (1, 0, 4, 3, 1, 0), p1 (1, 0, 1, 1, 1, 0), [p1, k5, p1] 2 (3, 4, 3, 4, 5, 6) times, p1 (1, 0, 1, 1, 1, 0), k2 (0, 0, 4, 2, 0, 0) (back/front), pm; rep from * once.

Setup Rnd 2: Work St st over sleeve sts, sm, k0 (2, 0, 2, 0, 2, 0), work Lace Pattern 3 (3, 4, 4, 5, 5, 6) times, k0 (1, 0, 1, 0, 1, 0) over back sts, sm, work St st over sleeve sts, sm, and k3 (1, 3, 1, 3, 1, 3), work Wide Garter Rib 2 (3, 3, 4, 4, 5, 5) times, k2 (0, 2, 0, 2, 0, 2) over front sts.

Note: From this point forward you will work sleeve sts in St st, back sts in Lace Pattern, and front sts in Wide Garter Rib. When working patt st sections (front and back) with increases, work new sts in established patt. If you find it difficult to work new sts in established patts, work in St st until you have enough sts to work patt sts.

Inc Rnd: K1, yo, work St st to 1 st before m, yo, k1, sm, k1, yo, work in established Lace Pattern to 1 st before m, yo, k1, sm, k1, yo, work St st to 1 st before m, yo, k1, sm, k1, yo, work in established Wide Garter Rib patt to 1 st before m, yo, k1—8 sts inc'd.

Working in established patts, rep Inc Rnd every other rnd 8 (10, 11, 13, 14, 16, 17) more times—136 (154, 166, 184, 204, 230, 248) sts total; 29 (31, 31, 33, 37, 43, 46) sts for each sleeve, 39 (46, 52, 59, 65, 72, 78) sts for each back and front.

Work even in established patts until yoke measures approximately 7.75 (8.25, 8.75, 9.25, 9.75, 10.5, 10.75) in. / 19.5 (21, 22, 23.5, 25, 26.5, 27.5) cm.

Lace Pattern

●						●	6
							5
●						●	4
			○	⋀	○		3
●						●	2
		○		⋀		○	1

☐ Knit

● Purl

○ yo

⋀ s2kp–sl2, k1, pass both sl sts over

☐ Repeat

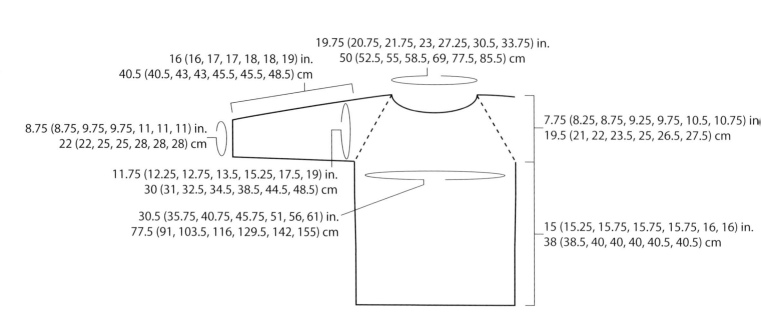

16 (16, 17, 17, 18, 18, 19) in.
40.5 (40.5, 43, 43, 45.5, 45.5, 48.5) cm

19.75 (20.75, 21.75, 23, 27.25, 30.5, 33.75) in.
50 (52.5, 55, 58.5, 69, 77.5, 85.5) cm

8.75 (8.75, 9.75, 9.75, 11, 11, 11) in.
22 (22, 25, 25, 28, 28, 28) cm

7.75 (8.25, 8.75, 9.25, 9.75, 10.5, 10.75) in.
19.5 (21, 22, 23.5, 25, 26.5, 27.5) cm

11.75 (12.25, 12.75, 13.5, 15.25, 17.5, 19) in.
30 (31, 32.5, 34.5, 38.5, 44.5, 48.5) cm

30.5 (35.75, 40.75, 45.75, 51, 56, 61) in.
77.5 (91, 103.5, 116, 129.5, 142, 155) cm

15 (15.25, 15.75, 15.75, 15.75, 16, 16) in.
38 (38.5, 40, 40, 40, 40.5, 40.5) cm

DIVIDE BODY AND SLEEVES

Division Rnd: Place 29 (31, 31, 33, 37, 43, 46) sleeve sts on waste yarn or st holder, CO 1 (1, 2, 2, 2, 2, 3) st(s), work Lace Pattern to next m, remove m, place 29 (31, 31, 33, 37, 43, 46) sleeve sts on waste yarn or st holder, CO 2 (2, 2, 2, 3, 3, 3) sts, pm, CO 1 (1, 2, 2, 2, 2, 3) st(s), work Wide Garter Rib patt to end of rnd, remove m, CO 2 (2, 2, 2, 3, 3, 3) sts, pm for new beg of rnd—84 (98, 112, 126, 140, 154, 168) sts.

BODY

Continue to work in established patts until body measures 12.75 (13, 13.5, 13.5, 13.5, 13.75, 13.75) in. / 32.5 (33, 34.5, 34.5, 34.5, 35, 35) cm, or approximately 2.25 in. / 5.5 cm less than desired length, ending on a Lace Pattern Row 6.

HEM

Ribbing Rnd: *(P1, k2) twice, p1; rep from * to end of rnd.
Rep last rnd 9 times.
BO all sts loosely in patt.

SLEEVES

Note: Sleeves are worked in the round. Use your favorite small circumference knitting needles and method.

Place 29 (31, 31, 33, 37, 43, 46) held sleeve sts back on the needle to work in the rnd, CO 1 (1, 2, 2, 2, 2, 3) st(s), knit sleeve sts, CO 2 (2, 2, 2, 3, 3, 3) sts, pm for beg of rnd—32 (34, 35, 37, 42, 48, 52) sts.

Work St st in the Rnd for 2 in. / 5 cm.
Dec Rnd: K1, k2tog, knit to end of rnd, ssk—2 sts dec'd.
Rep Dec Rnd every 11 (9, 11, 9, 8, 5, 4) rnds 3 (4, 3, 4, 5, 8, 10) more times—24 (24, 27, 27, 30, 30, 30) sts.
Work even until sleeve measures 14.5 (15, 15, 15.5, 15.5, 16, 16) in. / 37 (38, 38, 39.5, 39.5, 40.5, 40.5) cm, or approximately 2 in. / 5 cm less than desired length.

CUFF

Ribbing Rnd: *K2, p1; rep from * to end of rnd.
Rep last rnd 7 times.
BO all sts loosely in patt.
Rep for second sleeve.

FINISHING

Sew up underarms. Weave in ends. Block lightly to schematic measurements.

CHAPTER 5

Clever Cables

Cables are classic and timeless—and just the thing to bring your knitting up a notch. The perfectly placed cables on these sweaters will make them extra-special. Choose gorgeous yarns with depth and interest for these versatile wardrobe staples.

Delta

The beautiful golden hues of this yarn make a perfect backdrop for the intricate twisted stitch cables around the bottom border. Choose a hand-dyed yarn to make the reverse stockinette body pattern shine!

SIZE
Bust: 32 (36, 40, 44, 48, 52, 56) in. / 81.5 (91.5, 101.5, 112, 122, 132, 142) cm

YARN
Madelinetosh Dandelion; Fingering weight; 90% wool, 10% linen; 325 yd. / 297 m, 3.5 oz. / 100 g per skein
  Candlewick: 3 (3, 4, 4, 5, 5, 6) skeins

NEEDLES
US 3 (3.25 mm); adjust needle size as necessary to achieve gauge.

NOTIONS
- stitch markers
- cable needle
- tapestry needle
- waste yarn or stitch holders

GAUGE
28 sts and 38 rnds = 4 in. / 10 cm in rev St st

PATTERN STITCHES
Rev St st in the Rnd
  Rnd 1: Purl.
  Rep Rnd 1 for patt.
Twisted Rib
  Rnd 1: *K1tbl, p1tbl; rep from * to end.
  Rep Rnd 1 for patt.

SPECIAL ABBREVIATIONS
LT (left twist): Slip 2 sts knitwise, 1 at a time, to RH needle; slip back to LH needle, knit 2nd st through back loop, leaving st on needle, then knit both sts together through the back loops.
RT (right twist): K2tog, leaving sts on needle, knit 1st st again.

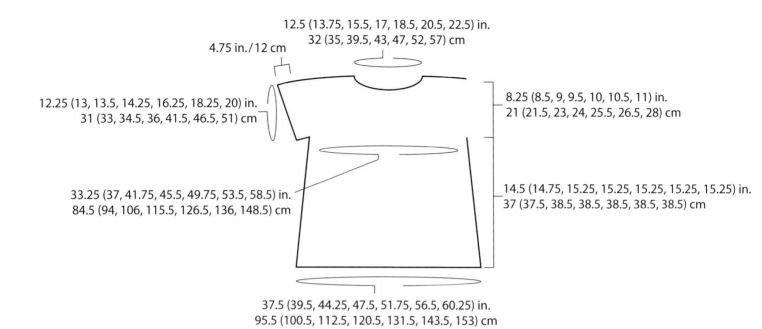

12.5 (13.75, 15.5, 17, 18.5, 20.5, 22.5) in.
32 (35, 39.5, 43, 47, 52, 57) cm

4.75 in./12 cm

12.25 (13, 13.5, 14.25, 16.25, 18.25, 20) in.
31 (33, 34.5, 36, 41.5, 46.5, 51) cm

8.25 (8.5, 9, 9.5, 10, 10.5, 11) in.
21 (21.5, 23, 24, 25.5, 26.5, 28) cm

33.25 (37, 41.75, 45.5, 49.75, 53.5, 58.5) in.
84.5 (94, 106, 115.5, 126.5, 136, 148.5) cm

14.5 (14.75, 15.25, 15.25, 15.25, 15.25, 15.25) in.
37 (37.5, 38.5, 38.5, 38.5, 38.5, 38.5) cm

37.5 (39.5, 44.25, 47.5, 51.75, 56.5, 60.25) in.
95.5 (100.5, 112.5, 120.5, 131.5, 143.5, 153) cm

Cable Chart

Legend:
- Knit (k)
- • Purl (p)
- V Slip wyib
- Right twist (RT)
- Left twist (LT)
- Knit tbl (k1tbl)
- p2tog
- M Make 1 (M1)
- Pattern repeat

NOTES

The main body of this sweater is worked in reverse stockinette—purl every round. If desired, the sweater can be worked inside out (knit every round) until the cabled bottom portion.

INSTRUCTIONS

YOKE

CO 160 (168, 172, 184, 192, 196, 204) sts. Pm and join to work in the rnd, being careful not to twist sts.

Work Twisted Rib for 12 rnds.

Setup Rnd: *P54 (60, 64, 70, 76, 80, 86), place raglan m, p26 (24, 22, 22, 20, 18, 16), place raglan m; rep from * once more.

Inc Rnd: *M1, purl to m, M1, sm; rep from * three times—8 sts inc'd.

Rep the Inc Rnd every other rnd 15 (21, 27, 32, 33, 41, 45) times—288 (344, 396, 448, 464, 532, 572) total sts; 86 (104, 120, 136, 144, 164, 178) sts for front/back and 58 (68, 78, 88, 88, 102, 108) sts for each sleeve.

Then rep the Inc Rnd every 4th round 10 (8, 6, 5, 7, 4, 3) times—368 (408, 444, 488, 520, 564, 596) total sts; 106 (120, 132, 146, 158, 172, 184) sts for front/back and 78 (84, 90, 98, 102, 110, 114) sts for each sleeve.

DIVIDE BODY AND SLEEVES

Knit to first m, remove m, sl next 78 (84, 90, 98, 102, 110, 114) sts to waste yarn or st holder for sleeve, remove m, CO 6 (6, 8, 8, 10, 10, 12) sts, knit to next m, remove m, sl next 78 (84, 90, 98, 102, 110, 114) sts to waste yarn or st holder for sleeve, remove m, CO 6 (6, 8, 8, 10, 10, 12) sts—224 (252, 280, 308, 336, 364, 392) body sts.

BODY

Work in Rev St st until body measures 14 in. / 35.5 cm, or 3 (3, 3, 4, 4, 5, 5) in. / 7.5 (7.5, 7.5, 10, 10, 12.5, 12.5) cm less than desired length.

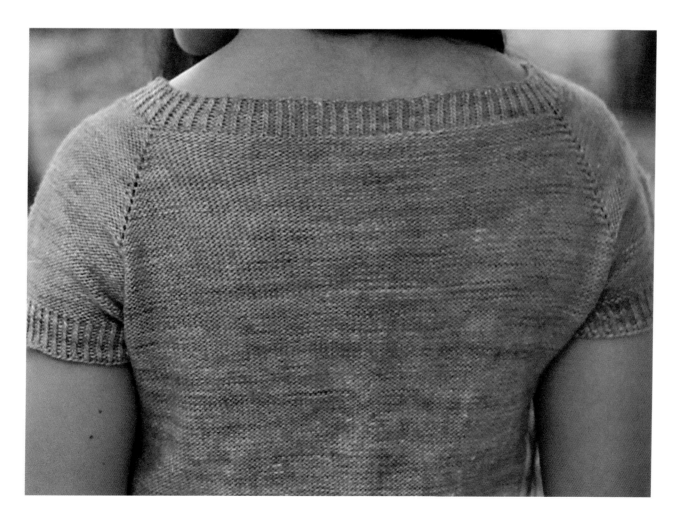

Inc Rnd: *P14 (21, 14, 19, 14, 18, 24), M1; rep from
* to last 0 (0, 0, 4, 0, 4, 8) sts, purl to end—
240 (264, 300, 324, 360, 384, 408) sts.
Work Rnds 1–20 of the Cable Chart once, work
Rnds 5–20 1 (1, 1, 2, 2, 3, 3) times, and then
work Rnds 21–22 once.
Work Twisted Rib for 12 rounds. BO all
sts loosely.

SLEEVES

Sleeves are worked in the round. Use your
favorite small circumference knitting needles
and method.

Place 78 (84, 90, 98, 102, 110, 114) held sleeve
sts back on the needles to work in the rnd. CO
3 (3, 4, 4, 5, 5, 6) sts, pm for beg of rnd, CO
3 (3, 4, 4, 5, 5, 6) sts, join for knitting in the
rnd—84 (90, 98, 106, 112, 120, 126) sts. Purl to m.
Purl 4 rnds.
Work Twisted Rib for 12 rnds.
BO all sts loosely.
Rep for second sleeve.

FINISHING

Seam up underarm seams. Weave in all ends.
Block lightly to schematic measurements.

Eudora

Time to get cozy. Stay warm in this bulky sweater with faux cables and garter ridge details. The Malabrigo Chunky yarn is pretty much the most delicious bulky out there, so you can't go wrong with this classic cardigan with A-line shaping.

SIZE
Bust without bands: 31.75 (35.75, 39.75, 43.75, 47.75, 51.75, 55.75) in. / 80.5 (91, 101, 111, 121.5, 131.5, 141.5) cm

Bust with bands buttoned: 33.75 (37.75, 41.75, 45.75, 49.75, 53.75, 57.75) in. / 85.5 (96, 106, 116, 126.5, 136.5, 146.5) cm

YARN
Malabrigo Chunky; Bulky weight; 100% merino wool; 100 yd. / 91 m, 3.5 oz. / 100 g per skein

Paris Night: 9 (10, 11, 12, 13, 14, 15) skeins

NEEDLES
US 11 (8.0 mm); adjust needle size as necessary to achieve gauge.

NOTIONS
- stitch markers
- tapestry needle
- waste yarn or stitch holders
- twelve 1-in. / 2.5-cm buttons

GAUGE
12 sts and 20 rows = 4 in. / 10 cm in St st

PATTERN STITCHES
St st Flat
  Row 1 (RS): Knit.
  Row 2 (WS): Purl.
  Rep Rows 1–2 for patt.
St st in the Rnd
  Rnd 1: Knit.
  Rep Rnd 1 for patt.
Garter st Flat
  Row 1: Knit.
  Rep Row 1 for patt.

INSTRUCTIONS

YOKE

CO 59 (59, 62, 62, 65, 65, 68) sts, do not join. Work St st Flat for 4 (6, 0, 0, 2, 4, 6) rows.

Work 3 (3, 4, 4, 4, 4, 4) reps of the 12-Row Cable Slip Pattern below, working the Inc Rows as directed on Row 1. For sizes 32 and 36, work Row 1 once more, working the Fourth Inc Row. For all other sizes, knit one more RS row.

12-ROW CABLE SLIP PATTERN

Row 1 (RS): Work next Inc Row as directed.
Row 2 (WS): Knit.
Row 3: K1, *sl 1, k2; rep from * to last st, k1.
Row 4: P1, *p2, sl 1; rep from * to last st, p1.
Row 5: K1, *drop sl st to front of work, k2, knit sl st; rep from * to last st, k1.
Row 6: Purl.
Row 7: K1, *yo, k2tog, k1; rep from * to last st, k1.
Row 8: Purl.
Row 9: K1, *k2, sl 1; rep from * to last st, k1.
Row 10: P1, *sl 1, p2; rep from * to last st, p1.
Row 11: K1, *sl 2, drop sl st to front of work, sl 2 sts back to LH needle, knit sl st, k2; rep from * to last st, k1.

Row 12: Knit.
Inc Row 1: K4 (3, 2, 15, 13, 12, 12), M1, *k3 (2, 2, 1, 1, 1, 1), M1; rep from * to last 4 (4, 2, 15, 14, 12, 12) sts, knit to end—77 (86, 92, 95, 104, 107, 113) sts.
Inc Row 2: K4 (4, 2, 12, 14, 12, 9), M1, *k3 (3, 3, 2, 2, 2, 2), M1; rep from * to last 4 (4, 3, 13, 14, 13, 10) sts, knit to end—101 (113, 122, 131, 143, 149, 161) sts.
Inc Row 3: K4 (4, 3, 13, 14, 8, 10), M1, *k4 (4, 4, 3, 3, 3, 3), M1; rep from * to last 5 (5, 3, 13, 15, 9, 10) sts, knit to end—125 (140, 152, 167, 182, 194, 209) sts.
Inc Row 4: K5 (5, 12, 13, 15, 9, 10), M1, *k5 (5, 4, 4, 4, 4, 4), M1; rep from * to last 5 (5, 12, 14, 15, 9, 11) sts, knit to end—149 (167, 185, 203, 221, 239, 257) sts.
Next Row (WS): Knit.

DIVIDE BODY AND SLEEVES

Dividing Row (RS): K21 (24, 27, 30, 33, 36, 39), place 33 (36, 39, 42, 45, 48, 51) sts on waste yarn or st holder for sleeve, CO 3 sts, pm, CO 3 sts, k41 (47, 53, 59, 65, 71, 77), place 33 (36, 39, 42, 45, 48, 51) sts on waste yarn or st holder for sleeve, CO 3 sts, pm, CO 3 sts, knit to end—95 (107, 119, 131, 143, 155, 167) sts.

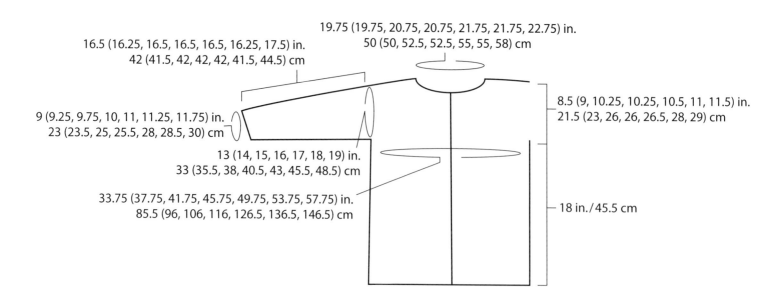

19.75 (19.75, 20.75, 20.75, 21.75, 21.75, 22.75) in.
50 (50, 52.5, 52.5, 55, 55, 58) cm

16.5 (16.25, 16.5, 16.5, 16.5, 16.25, 17.5) in.
42 (41.5, 42, 42, 42, 41.5, 44.5) cm

8.5 (9, 10.25, 10.25, 10.5, 11, 11.5) in.
21.5 (23, 26, 26, 26.5, 28, 29) cm

9 (9.25, 9.75, 10, 11, 11.25, 11.75) in.
23 (23.5, 25, 25.5, 28, 28.5, 30) cm

13 (14, 15, 16, 17, 18, 19) in.
33 (35.5, 38, 40.5, 43, 45.5, 48.5) cm

33.75 (37.75, 41.75, 45.75, 49.75, 53.75, 57.75) in.
85.5 (96, 106, 116, 126.5, 136.5, 146.5) cm

18 in./45.5 cm

BODY

Next Row (WS): Purl.

BODY PATTERN

Beg with Row 7 (9, 3, 3, 5, 7, 9) of the Body Pattern work in patt until body measures approximately 15 in. / 38 cm, or 3 in. / 7.5 cm less than desired length—119 (135, 143, 155, 167, 179, 195) sts. Work Garter St for 24 rows. BO all sts loosely.

Row 1 (RS): Knit.

Row 2 (WS): Purl.

Rows 3–8: Rep Rows 1–2.

Row 9: Knit.

Row 10: Knit to 1 st before next m, M1, k1, sm, k1, M1, knit to 1 st before next m, M1, k1, sm, k1, M1, knit to end—4 sts inc'd.

Rows 11–12: Knit.

SLEEVES

Note: Sleeves are worked in the round. Use your favorite small circumference knitting needles and method.

Place 33 (36, 39, 42, 45, 48, 51) sts back on needles to work in the rnd. CO 4 sts, pm for beg of rnd, CO 2 sts—39 (42, 45, 48, 51, 54, 57) sts. Work the 12-Rnd Sleeve Pattern below, decreasing 2 sts every 12 (10, 9, 8, 8, 7, 7)th rnd 6 (7, 8, 9, 9, 10, 11) times using the Dec Rnd below—27 (28, 29, 30, 33, 34, 35) sts. When working shaping, be sure to maintain proper st count in the sleeve pattern by pairing each patterned yo with its corresponding decrease. If this is not possible because of the current st count, work in St st instead.

Dec Rnd: Work in patt for 1 st, k2tog, work in patt to last 3 sts, ssk, work in patt for 1 st—2 sts dec'd.

12-RND SLEEVE PATTERN

Rnds 1–2: *Sl 1, k2; rep from * to end.

Rnd 3: K1, *drop sl st to front of work, k2, knit sl st; rep from * to last st, k1.

Rnd 4: Knit.

Rnd 5: *Yo, k2tog, k1; rep from * to end.

Rnd 6: Knit.

Rnd 7: *K2, sl 1; rep from * to end.

Rnd 8: *Sl 1, p2; rep from * to end.

Rnd 9: *Sl 2, drop sl st to front of work, sl 2 sts back to LH needle, knit sl st, k2; rep from * to end.

Rnd 10: Purl.

Rnd 11: Knit.

Rnd 12: Purl.

CUFF

Rnd 1: Purl.

Rnd 2: Knit.

Rep last 2 rnds 4 more times. Purl 1 rnd. BO all sts loosely.

Rep for second sleeve.

FINISHING

COLLAR

With WS facing, pick up and knit 59 (59, 62, 62, 65, 65, 68) sts from the neck CO.

Next Row (WS): Knit.

Inc Row (RS): K1, *M1, k2; rep from * to last 0 (0, 1, 1, 0, 0, 1) sts, M1, k0 (0, 1, 1, 0, 0, 1)—89 (89, 93, 93, 98, 98, 102) sts.

Work Garter st for 4 in. / 10 cm.

BO all sts loosely.

BUTTONBAND

With RS of Right Front facing and beg at bottom of Right Front working toward Collar, pick up and knit about 2 sts for every 3 rows along Right Front edge; then pick up and knit 1 st for each ridge of the Collar. Work Garter St for 11 rows. BO all sts loosely.

BUTTONHOLE BAND

Mark placement of 12 buttonholes on Left Front, the lowest 1 in. / 2.5 cm from bottom edge, the highest 1 in. / 2.5 cm from top edge of the collar, and the remaining 10 evenly spaced in between.

With RS of Left Front facing and beg at top of Collar working toward bottom of Left Front, pick up and knit 1 st for each ridge of the Collar; then pick up and knit about 2 sts for every 3 rows along Left Front edge. Work Garter St for 5 rows.

Buttonhole Row (RS): Knit, BO 2 sts opposite each marked buttonhole position.

Next Row (WS): Knit, CO 2 over each buttonhole.

Cont in Garter St for 4 more rows. BO all sts loosely.

Sew up underarms. Weave in ends. Block lightly to schematic measurements.

Glenda

Openwork cables make up the gorgeous top of this knitted tee. Reverse stockinette in the body and rolled hems make it unique and easy to wear!

SIZE
Bust: 32 (37.5, 41.5, 50.5, 52.75, 56.75, 62.5) in. / 81.5 (95.5, 105.5, 128.5, 134, 144, 159) cm

YARN
Knit Picks Swish DK; DK weight; 100% superwash merino wool; 123 yd. / 112 m, 1.8 oz. / 50 g per skein
  Honey: 7 (9, 10, 12, 13, 14, 16) skeins

NEEDLES
US 7 (4.5 mm); adjust needle size as necessary to achieve gauge.

NOTIONS
- stitch markers
- tapestry needle
- waste yarn or stitch holder
- cable needle

GAUGE
20 sts and 28 rnds = 4 in. / 10 cm in rev St st

PATTERN STITCHES
St st in the Rnd
  Rnd 1: Knit.
  Rep Rnd 1 for patt.
Rev St st in the Rnd
  Rnd 1: Purl.
  Rep Rnd 1 for patt.

SPECIAL ABBREVIATIONS
2/2 RPC: Slip 2 sts to cable needle, hold to back, k2, p2 from cable needle.
2/2 LPC: Slip 2 sts to cable needle, hold to front, p2, k2 from cable needle.

INSTRUCTIONS

YOKE

CO 116 (124, 124, 132, 132, 140, 140) sts, pm, and join to work in the rnd.

Setup Rnd: *K20 (22, 22, 24, 24, 26, 26), pm, K38 (40, 40, 42, 42, 44, 44), pm; rep from * once more.

Work St st in the Rnd for 7 rnds.

Each size works a different combination of the charts as follows:

*Work Chart indicated, sm; rep from * 3 times.

Size 32 Only
Chart A: Rnds 1-50—236 sts.
Chart C: Rnds 1-6—244 sts.

Size 37.5 only
Chart B: Rnds 3-22—212 sts.
Chart A: Rnds 47-64—252 sts.
Chart A: Rnds 1-18—300 sts.
Chart D: Rnds 1-6—308 sts.

Size 41.5 only
Chart B: Rnds 3-22—212 sts.
Chart A: Rnds 47-64—252 sts.
Chart A: Rnds 1-22—308 sts.
Chart E: Rnds 1-6—316 sts.

Size 50.5 only
Chart B: Rnds 5-32—260 sts.
Chart B: Rnds 1-8—300 sts.
Chart A: Rnds 17-42—372 sts.
Chart F: Rnds 1-6—380 sts.

Size 52.75 only
Chart B: Rnds 5-32—260 sts.
Chart B: Rnds 1-24—372 sts.
Chart A: Rnds 49-62—404 sts.
Chart G: Rnds 1-6—412 sts.

Size 56.75 only
Chart B: Rnds 7-32—260 sts.
Chart B: Rnds 1-28—388 sts.
Chart A: Rnds 25-42—428 sts.
Chart F: Rnds 1-6—436 sts.

Size 62.5 only
Chart B: Rnds 7-32—260 sts.
Chart B: Rnds 1-32—404 sts.
Chart B: Rnds 1-12—460 sts.
Chart A: Rnds 57-62—476 sts.
Chart G: Rnds 1-6—484 sts.

All Sizes
244 (308, 316, 380, 412, 436, 484) sts; 52 (68, 70, 86, 94, 100, 112) sts for each sleeve and 70 (86, 88, 104, 112, 118, 130) sts for each front/back.

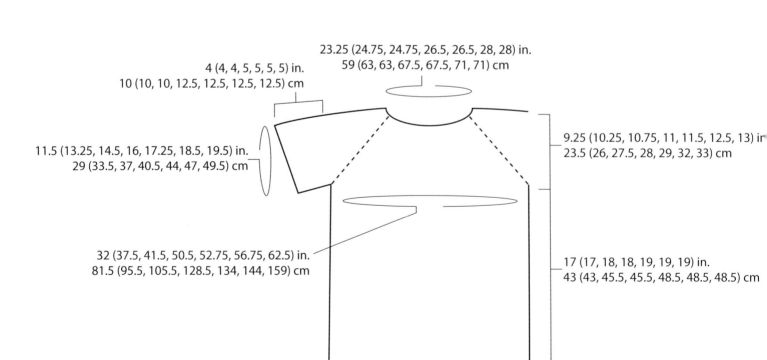

23.25 (24.75, 24.75, 26.5, 26.5, 28, 28) in.
59 (63, 63, 67.5, 67.5, 71, 71) cm

4 (4, 4, 5, 5, 5, 5) in.
10 (10, 10, 12.5, 12.5, 12.5, 12.5) cm

9.25 (10.25, 10.75, 11, 11.5, 12.5, 13) in
23.5 (26, 27.5, 28, 29, 32, 33) cm

11.5 (13.25, 14.5, 16, 17.25, 18.5, 19.5) in.
29 (33.5, 37, 40.5, 44, 47, 49.5) cm

32 (37.5, 41.5, 50.5, 52.75, 56.75, 62.5) in.
81.5 (95.5, 105.5, 128.5, 134, 144, 159) cm

17 (17, 18, 18, 19, 19, 19) in.
43 (43, 45.5, 45.5, 48.5, 48.5, 48.5) cm

Chart A

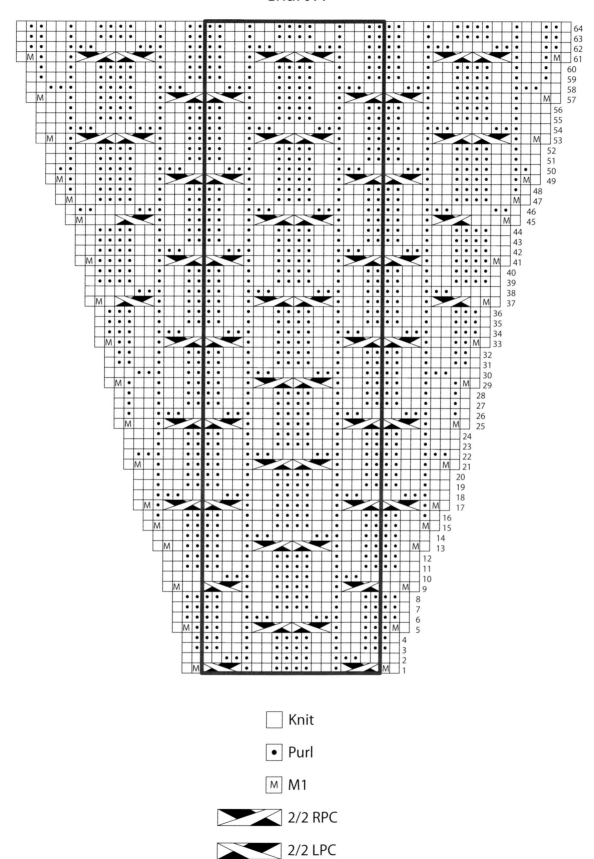

☐ Knit

• Purl

Ⓜ M1

◣◥ 2/2 RPC

◤◢ 2/2 LPC

Chart B

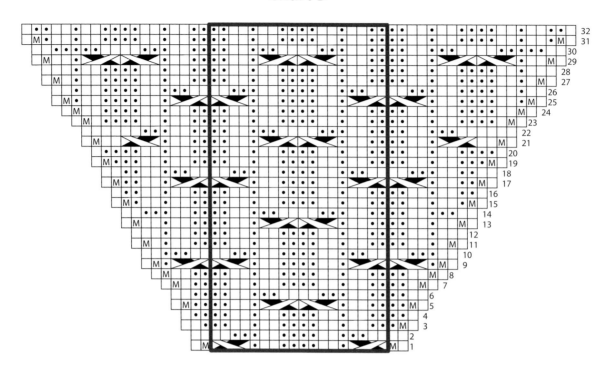

Chart C

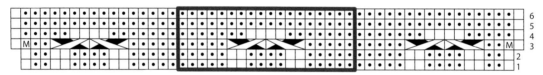

Chart D

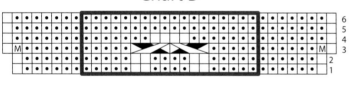

Chart E

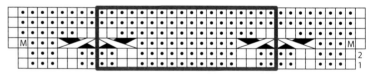

Chart F

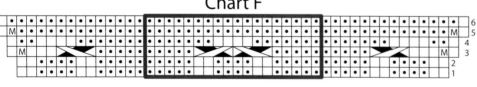

Chart G

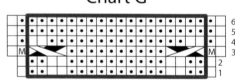

	Knit
•	Purl
M	M1
	2/2 RPC
	2/2 LPC

DIVIDE BODY AND SLEEVES

Dividing Rnd: Remove m, p 1 (2, 3, 7, 7, 8, 10), place next 50 (63, 63, 72, 80, 84, 92) sts on waste yarn or st holder for sleeve, CO 4 (2, 5, 4, 3, 4, 3) sts, place beg of rnd m, CO 4 (1, 4, 4, 3, 4, 3) sts, purl to next m, remove m, purl to next m, remove m, p1 (2, 3, 7, 7, 8, 10), place next 50 (63, 63, 72, 80, 84, 92) sts on waste yarn or st holder for sleeve, CO 8 (3, 9, 8, 6, 8, 6) sts, purl to next m, remove m, purl to end of rnd—160 (188, 208, 252, 264, 284, 312) sts for body.

BODY

Work in the rnd in Rev St st in the Rnd until Body measures 16 (16, 17, 17, 18, 18, 18) in. / 40.5 (40.5, 43, 43, 45.5, 45.5, 45.5) cm from underarm. (If desired, turn sweater inside out to knit the body in St st in the Rnd.) Work St st in the Rnd for 8 rnds. BO all sts loosely.

SLEEVES

Note: Sleeves are worked in the round. Use your favorite small circumference knitting needles and method.

Place 50 (63, 63, 72, 80, 84, 92) held sleeve sts back on needle to work in the rnd, CO 4 (2, 5, 4, 3, 4, 3) sts, place beg of rnd m, CO 4 (1, 4, 4, 3, 4, 3) sts—58 (66, 72, 80, 86, 92, 98) sts. Work Rev St st in the rnd until sleeve measures 3 (3, 3, 4, 4, 4, 4) in. / 7.5 (7.5, 7.5, 10, 10, 10, 10) cm from underarm.

Work St st in the Rnd for 8 rnds. BO all sts loosely.

Rep for second sleeve.

FINISHING

Sew up underarms. Weave in ends. Block lightly to schematic measurements.

Lenora

Knit yourself up a warm and woolly layering piece in no time in squishy, bulky merino. Choose a statement button (you just need one!) to make this a stylish wear-everywhere knit.

SIZE
Bust: 32 (36, 40, 44, 48, 52, 56) in. / 81.5 (91.5, 101.5, 112, 122, 132, 142) cm

YARN
Stitch Sprouts Crater Lake; Bulky weight; 100% merino wool; 110 yd. / 100 m, 3.5 oz. / 100 g per skein
   Wizard Island: 4 (5, 6, 6, 7, 8, 9) skeins

NEEDLES
US 10.5 (6.5 mm); adjust needle size as necessary to achieve gauge.

NOTIONS
- stitch markers
- tapestry needle
- cable needle
- one 1-in. / 2.5-cm button

GAUGE
14 sts and 20 rows = 4 in. / 10 cm in St st

SPECIAL ABBREVIATIONS
3/3 LC: Slip 3 sts to cable needle and hold to front, k3, k3 sts from cable needle.

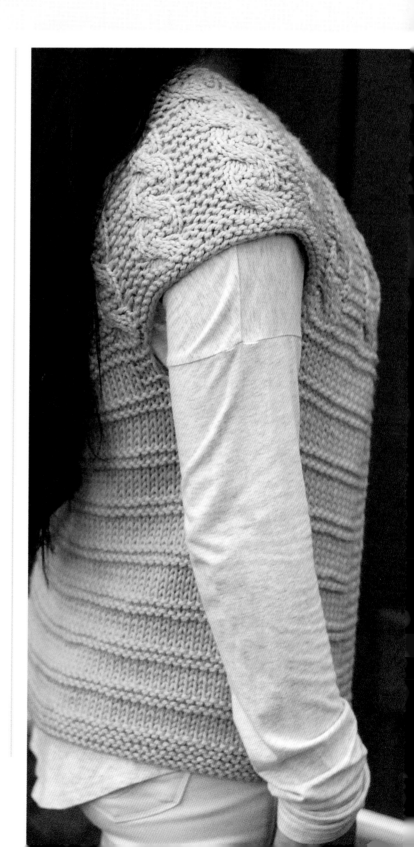

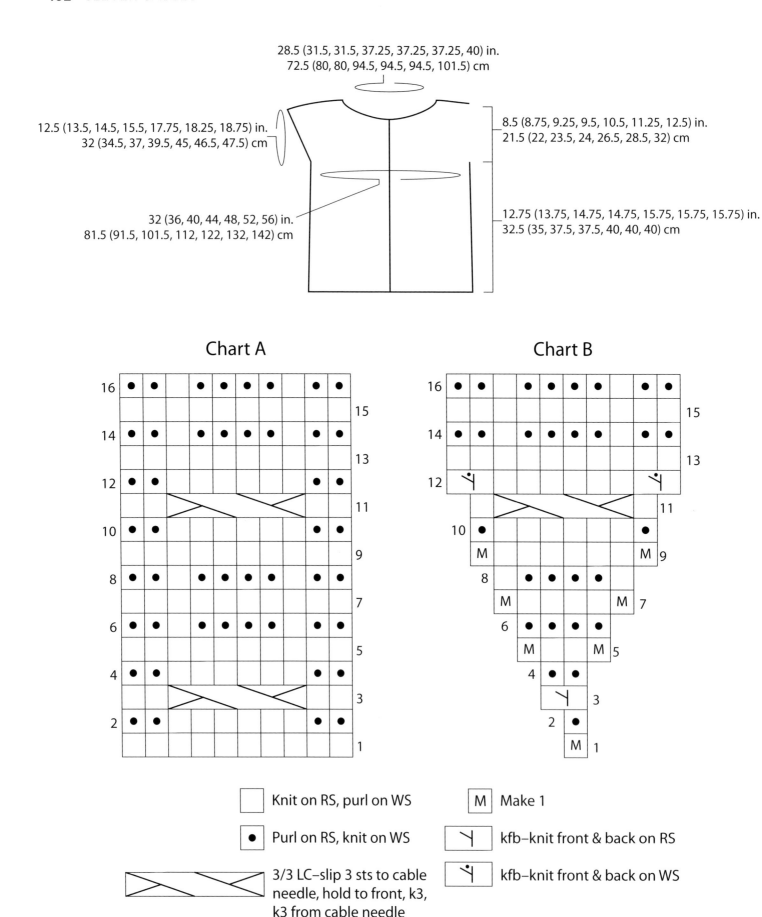

28.5 (31.5, 31.5, 37.25, 37.25, 37.25, 40) in.
72.5 (80, 80, 94.5, 94.5, 94.5, 101.5) cm

12.5 (13.5, 14.5, 15.5, 17.75, 18.25, 18.75) in.
32 (34.5, 37, 39.5, 45, 46.5, 47.5) cm

8.5 (8.75, 9.25, 9.5, 10.5, 11.25, 12.5) in.
21.5 (22, 23.5, 24, 26.5, 28.5, 32) cm

32 (36, 40, 44, 48, 52, 56) in.
81.5 (91.5, 101.5, 112, 122, 132, 142) cm

12.75 (13.75, 14.75, 14.75, 15.75, 15.75, 15.75) in.
32.5 (35, 37.5, 37.5, 40, 40, 40) cm

Chart A

Chart B

Knit on RS, purl on WS

● Purl on RS, knit on WS

3/3 LC–slip 3 sts to cable
needle, hold to front, k3,
k3 from cable needle

M Make 1

Y kfb–knit front & back on RS

Y kfb–knit front & back on WS

INSTRUCTIONS

COLLAR

CO 100 (110, 110, 130, 130, 130, 140) sts.
Row 1 (WS): Sl 1, knit to end.
Rows 2–3: Rep Row 1.
Row 4: Sl 1, k2, BO 2 sts, knit to end.
Row 5: Sl 1, knit to buttonhole, CO 2 sts, knit to end.

YOKE

Work Charts A and B as follows: 160 (180, 190, 210, 220, 230, 240) sts.
   All Rows: Sl 1, k4, work chart sequence for your size as listed below, k5.
   Size 32: A, A, (B, A) 6 times, A.
   Size 36: A, A, (B, A) 7 times, A.
   Size 40: A, (B, A) 4 times, A, (B, A) 4 times.
   Size 44: A, A, (B, A) 4 times, A, A, (B, A) 4 times.
   Size 48: A, A, (B, A) 9 times, A.
   Size 52: A, (B, A) 5 times, A, (B, A) 5 times.
   Size 56: A, A, (B, A) 10 times, A.

All Sizes

Cont working just Chart A as follows:
Next Row: Sl 1, k4, work Chart A to last 5 sts, k5.
Rep last row 15 (17, 19, 21, 25, 29, 35) more times.

TRANSITION ROWS

Row 1 (RS): Sl 1, knit to end.
Rows 2–4: Rep Row 1.
Row 5: Sl 1, k22 (26, 28, 31, 32, 36, 37), BO 34 (37, 38, 41, 44, 44, 44) sts, k46 (52, 56, 64, 66, 68, 76), BO 34 (37, 38, 41, 44, 44, 44) sts, knit to end—92 (106, 114, 128, 132, 142, 152) sts.
Row 6: Sl 1, k4, p14 (18, 20, 23, 24, 28, 29), k4, CO 10 (10, 13, 13, 18, 20, 22) sts, k4, p38 (44, 48, 56, 58, 60, 68), k4, CO 10 (10, 13, 13, 18, 20, 22) sts, k4, purl to last 5 sts, k5.
Row 7: Sl 1, knit to end—112 (126, 140, 154, 168, 182, 196) sts.
Row 8: Sl 1, k4, p14 (18, 20, 23, 24, 28, 29), k18 (18, 21, 21, 26, 28, 30), p38 (44, 48, 56, 58, 60, 68), k18 (18, 21, 21, 26, 28, 30), purl to last 5 sts, k5.

BODY

BODY PATTERN

Row 1 (RS): Sl 1, knit to end.
Rows 2-5: Rep Row 1.
Row 6: Sl 1, k4, purl to last 5 sts, k5.
Row 7: Rep Row 1.
Row 8: Rep Row 6.
Rep last 8 Rows until body measures 11 (12, 13, 13, 14, 14, 14) in. / 28 (30.5, 33, 33, 35.5, 35.5, 35.5) cm from underarm or until 1.75 in. / 4.5 cm less than desired body length ending with a WS row.

HEM

Row 1 (RS): Sl 1, knit to end.
Rows 2-8: Rep Row 1.
BO all sts loosely.

FINISHING

Weave in all ends. Block lightly to schematic measurements. Sew button to collar opposite buttonhole.

Abbreviations

2/2 LPC: slip 2 sts purlwise to cable needle, hold to front of work, p2, k2 sts from cable needle

2/2 RPC: slip 2 sts purlwise to cable needle, hold to back of work, k2, p2 sts from cable needle

3/3 LC: slip 3 sts purlwise to cable needle, hold to front of work, k3, k3 sts from cable needle

beg: beginning

BO: bind off

c3 (cluster 3): slip 1 st purlwise, k2, pass slip stitch over both—1 st dec'd

CC: contrast color

CO: cast on

cont: continue; continued

dec('d): decrease(d)

inc('d): increase(d)

k: knit

k1tbl: knit 1 through back loop

k2tog: knit 2 sts together—1 st dec'd

kfb: knit into front and back of same st—1 st inc'd

kwise: knitwise

kyok (knit, yarn over, knit): (k1, yo, k1) in same st—2 sts inc'd

LH: left hand

LT (left twist): slip 2 sts knitwise, 1 at a time, to RH needle; slip back to LH needle, knit 2nd st through back loop, leaving st on needle, then knit both sts together through the back loops

m: marker

M1 (make 1): insert LH needle from front to back under horizontal strand between last st worked and next st on LH needle, knit through back of resulting loop—1 st inc'd

MC: main color

p: purl

p1tbl: purl 1 through back loop

p2tog: purl 2 together—1 st dec'd

patt(s): pattern(s)

pfb: purl into front and back of same st—1 st inc'd

pm: place marker

pwise: purlwise

rep: repeat

Rev St st: reverse stockinette stitch

rnd(s): round(s)

RH: right hand

RS: right side

RT (right twist): k2tog, leaving sts on needle, knit 1st st again

s2kp: slip 2 sts together knitwise, k1, pass both slip sts over—2 sts dec'd

sl: slip

sm: slip marker

ssk: slip the next 2 sts, knitwise, 1 at a time, to RH needle; slip back to LH needle without twisting and knit them together through the back loop—1 st dec'd

St st: stockinette stitch

st(s): stitch(es)

tog: together

WS: wrong side

wyib: with yarn in back

wyif: with yarn in front

yo (yarn over): bring yarn to the front, wrap it over the top of the RH needle, and work next stitch

Yarn Sources

Anzula
anzula.com

Baah
baahyarn.com

Berroco
berroco.com

Crabapple Yarns
crabappleyarns.com

Fiber Seed
thefiberseed.com

Knit Picks
knitpicks.com

Madelinetosh
madelinetosh.com

Malabrigo
malabrigoyarn.com

Mrs. Crosby
mrscrosbyplays.com

Patons
yarnspirations.com/patons

Stitch Sprouts
stitchsprouts.com

Sweet Georgia
sweetgeorgiayarns.com

Acknowledgments

With special thanks to my sample knitters: Brenda Pirie, Chaitanya Muralidhara, Chris Gagnon, Dolly Quinn, Heather Risher, Karen Verbenko, Kari Bhana, Kelly Asfour, Kristin Bellehumeur, and Stacie Berard. I could have not done this book without your nimble fingers.

To my tech editors Heather Anne Zoppetti and Britt Schmiesing, thank you for making the numbers make sense and helping me through this crazy process.

To my friends and colleagues who cheered me along the way—with special thanks to Angela Tong, Dawn Frazier, and Rose Tussing for your support toward the end, when life began to throw me all the curveballs.

Visual Index

Tantalizing Texture

Auralee
6

Shanna
14

Beryl
18

Rhoda
24

Captivating Colorwork

Vivian
32

Maude
38

Zelma
44

Trudy
50

Lovely and Lacy

Idabelle
58

Flora
64

Odette
70

Constance
76

Clever Cables

Delta
82

Eudora
88

Glenda
94

Lenora
100